Early praise for *Practical Security*

Figuring out where to begin securing systems can seem like an insurmountable task. *Practical Security* lays out the basics of how to handle high-risk areas so that small organizations and developers can start their security journey.

➤ **Michael C. Brown**
Senior Security Engineer

This book has the most down-to-earth, actionable advice for anyone who connects their valuables to the internet, from very small companies to the largest. While it's pretty tough to make anything connected to your organization totally safe, following the practices in this book will significantly raise the cost to attackers.

➤ **William Lederer**
President, CIEX, Inc.

A lot of security resources are targeted toward people who already know a lot about security, leaving a big gap for others who want to know how to keep their computers and networks safe. Roman provides accessible and practical advice that anyone can follow to get started.

➤ **Cade Cairns**
Security Engineer

A good overview of important topics when getting started with security in a small organization, complete with in-depth explanations of common issues and pointers to additional resources.

➤ **aschmitz**
Principal Security Consultant

This book is an excellent introduction to some of the topics you need to be a secure software engineer. It is pleasurable to read and well written.

➤ **Adam Ringwood**
Threat Research Engineer

Practical Security

Simple Practices for Defending Your Systems

Roman Zabicki

The Pragmatic Bookshelf

Raleigh, North Carolina

Our Pragmatic books, screencasts, and audio books can help you and your team create better software and have more fun. Visit us at *https://pragprog.com*.

The team that produced this book includes:

Publisher: Andy Hunt
VP of Operations: Janet Furlow
Managing Editor: Susan Conant
Development Editor: Adaobi Obi Tulton
Copy Editor: Molly McBeath
Layout: Gilson Graphics

For sales, volume licensing, and support, please contact *support@pragprog.com*.

For international rights, please contact *rights@pragprog.com*.

ISBN-13: 978-1-68050-634-1
Book version: P1.0—February 2019

To Marnie

Thanks for all the geek time

Contents

Acknowledgments

First of all, thank you to my wife, Marnie, for all the geek time you gave me to finish this book. I appreciate all your patience.

Thank you to my editor, Adaobi. You answered so many questions and gave me a lot of good advice on making this book more readable.

Thank you to Security Bill for taking a chance on me and giving me my first job in computer security. From watching the movie *Sneakers* to this, it's been a blast.

Thank you to the Pragmatic Bookshelf for agreeing to publish my book. I never thought I'd be a published author some day.

Thank you to the Chicago Public Library. In particular, thank you to the Harold Washington and Conrad Sulzer branches. You gave me a nice, quiet place to write. You're a place where I can sit for hours without feeling rushed or that I need to spend money. My mom took us to the Sulzer often when we were kids, and I loved to sit in the giant throne-like chairs and read. Going back to the Sulzer to write was a treat. You're a treasure for the city.

Thank you, Mom. You've always had a big pile of books waiting to be read, and you've always had a couple of writing projects going at any given time. Great Scott, that must have planted a seed in my mind!

Thank you to all of my reviewers. This book is a lot better because you took the time to review it. I was impressed by your attention to details both technical and aesthetic. In no particular order, thank you to Jeffery Stanford, Bill Lederer, Laurens Van Houtven, Adam Ringwood, Dominic Le, Scott Horowitz, Ben Sweet, Cade Cairns, Chris Wilken, Michael C. Brown, Joni Musa, Chris Walsh, and aschmitz.

I'm not unique in relying on my spouse, editor, and reviewers. I am, however, uniquely lucky to have you in particular to lean on. Thank you, all.

Introduction

It seems like hardly a week goes by without a high-profile computer breach. Why do these happen? How can you prevent them? This book doesn't have all the answers, but it does outline practices that make life harder for attackers and that help tide you over until you get a full-time security team in place.

This book is about getting the security basics right when you're starting out (or if you've been at it a while but haven't had guidance). There's no getting around the need for bringing on full-time security staff and outside security consultants as your organization gets more mature. Lots of complex security decisions require the judgment of a professional who has the full context of your particular situation. But if you have the basics taken care of, you'll free up the experts to take on harder problems and you'll get more out of them.

When you first bring in security consultants, you may only have a budget for one engagement per year. That's your one shot to learn from these experts. They'll happily report on the kinds of things outlined in this book. But that will eat up the time allocated for the engagement. You'll have spent your budget, and you'll have to wait another year before you get a chance to learn anything else from them. Don't spend a year and tens of thousands of dollars to learn the things that you could learn in a week by reading this book.

Who Is This Book For?

This book is for developers, admins, team leads, architects, technology generalists, and all others who stand guard against the things that go bump in the network. It's particularly for those who work in organizations that don't have dedicated security staff or don't have much interaction with dedicated security staff. If you thought that a couple of those job titles could apply to you, this book is for you. Sometimes these kinds of organizations are startups. Sometimes they're software development teams in large, well-established companies who have been left on their own to determine their own security posture alongside their regular day job of building useful software systems.

What's in This Book

This book covers five basic practices to improve your security posture.

Start with Chapter 1, *Patching*, on page 1. What happens when a serious vulnerability makes headlines? You need to quickly and authoritatively discover whether you use that software and then patch it if needed. Hopefully you have this capability today. If not, you can build up the capability to respond to this scenario now, when you're not rushed, when you can plan, prioritize, and test the work just like any other engineering work. Or you can wait until it's an emergency.

Next, you'll explore some basic software vulnerabilities in Chapter 2, *Vulnerabilities*, on page 23. You'll see how they work, how to prevent them, and, in some cases, how to make attempts to exploit them more detectable. You'll also learn about some common misconfigurations that can take otherwise secure software and open it up to attack.

You've probably heard the advice "Never write your own crypto." In Chapter 3, *Cryptography*, on page 55, you'll find out why this is good advice. You'll also discover some cryptography libraries you can use instead.

Odds are you have a lot of Windows computers in your organization. In Chapter 4, *Windows*, on page 83, you'll learn about configuration choices you can make to keep your Windows computers more secure.

Finally, in Chapter 5, *Phishing*, on page 93, you'll see what phishing is and what attackers typically try to achieve with phishing emails. You'll learn what your organization should cover in its phishing training and what defenses you can put in place to make your organizations more resistant to phishing attacks.

Online Resources

The book's website has the source code for this book.[1] You can also use the book's website to post errata in case you find any issues while reading the book.

Now let's dig in and start making your organization more secure.

---

1. https://pragprog.com/book/rzsecur/pragmatic-security

CHAPTER 1

Patching

Let's pretend that every piece of software that your organization ever writes from here on out is completely perfect. All of your developers are attentive and well trained. Your developers will never write code with a logic error, SQL injection, or cross-site scripting vulnerability. (Don't worry if you don't know what these vulnerabilities are yet.)

Aaah. Safe, cozy, and warm. It feels good to know that we're completely secure, doesn't it?

Nope.

Even if all the code that *you* write is perfect, you're still at risk. You're dependent on lots of software written by third parties. We don't know what vulnerabilities exist in third-party software, when these vulnerabilities will become public, or when patches will become available.

What's worse, this state of ignorance is time critical. Once a vulnerability is made public, security researchers and criminals alike start writing tools to scan for vulnerable computers. Scanning tools allow attackers to find your vulnerable public systems even if they'd never had any reason to attack you before. The internet makes every public-facing computer equally close. Even if the technical details of a vulnerability are not made public and only a patch is made available, motivated attackers can look at what's changed to try to find likely attack vectors. As defenders, it's important that we learn to use these tools to help us find our own vulnerable systems before criminals do.

Upgrading Third-Party Libraries and Software

When defending ourselves against the risks implicit in third-party libraries, we need to know what third-party software we use, and it takes a surprisingly large amount of effort to discover this. Once we know what's in use, we need the ability to quickly upgrade any of the third-party libraries and any software deployed in our organization. What's more, we need to be able to test these upgrades so that we can have confidence that the upgrade won't break anything. We'll want to automate this as much as possible because we need to do it often and we need to do it correctly. Manual upgrades done infrequently are unlikely to work when applied under extreme stress and at the hurried pace likely to accompany a newly discovered and critical vulnerability. Finally, we need to be able to do it on short notice because we don't know when we'll need to upgrade.

In order to be ready to upgrade, we need to be relatively current with our dependencies. We can't remain on old, unsupported versions of software, even if the old versions are functionally sufficient. Being out-of-date is likely to cause trouble when a vulnerability is found. If we're a couple years out-of-date on a library and a vulnerability is announced in that library, we risk that the fix for that vulnerability will only be available in the latest version of the library. There could be breaking changes between our old, vulnerable version of that library and the current version. This puts us in a bad situation, where we're unable to upgrade to a fixed version, even though we know there is a vulnerability in the version we're using.

We'll start by looking at patching and then look at the impact of a real-life patching mistake. Then we'll take an inventory of three kinds of third-party software that we use—libraries we build our software with, networked software listening on our network, and operating systems. Inventory in hand, we'll look at how to find published vulnerabilities in that software. We'll wrap up the chapter by outlining the testing we'll need to have in place in order to upgrade quickly.

A Closer Look at Patching

Patching is the broccoli and spinach and push-ups of security. It's not glamorous. You won't get to do a talk at a prestigious conference from it. You'll never be finished, either. But it's one of the fundamental practices you need in place to keep the bad guys out.

Patching is the ongoing practice of the following:

1. Looking at what software you have in place

2. Researching what vulnerabilities have been discovered in that software

3. Upgrading the vulnerable software to secure versions

4. Testing to make sure that the new versions work

This defense is a lot of work, but what's nice about it is that we don't have to become security experts overnight to implement it. We just need to be experts in our own systems.

Patching and the Equifax Breach

One of the most widely discussed breaches of 2017 was the Equifax breach, in which hackers accessed the sensitive personal information of approximately 145.5 million Americans.[1] We can learn a lot about the importance of patch management by looking at this breach. Equifax has shared a lot of information related to the breach in its September 15, 2017, press release, including a timeline.[2] Equifax has determined that the cause of the breach was a vulnerability in Apache Struts. This vulnerability allowed attackers to run arbitrary commands on the vulnerable server with the privileges of the Apache process itself.[3]

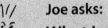

Joe asks:

What Is a CVE?

CVE stands for common vulnerabilities and exposures. It is the closest thing the field has to a centralized repository of vulnerabilities. Many operating system vendors and large software vendors track their own security vulnerabilities in the public CVE list. But there is no requirement for anyone to use the CVE system. As you continue to search for vulnerabilities in your dependencies over time, you'll start to develop an intuition for which vendors use CVE and which don't.

For more details about the CVE system as well as a searchable web interface, go to the CVE website.[a]

---

a.   cve.mitre.org

Now let's look at the timeline.

- March 2, 2017—Struts development team released a patch to fix this issue.[4]

- March 7, 2017—Payload to exploit this vulnerability was added to Metasploit.[5]

---

1.   https://www.equifaxsecurity2017.com/
2.   https://investor.equifax.com/news-and-events/news/2017/09-15-2017-224018832
3.   https://nvd.nist.gov/vuln/detail/CVE-2017-5638
4.   https://cwiki.apache.org/confluence/pages/viewpage.action?pageId=68717750
5.   https://github.com/rapid7/metasploit-framework/issues/8064

- March 9, 2017—Dan Goodin wrote an article describing this vulnerability on Ars Technica.[6]

- March 10, 2017—This vulnerability was assigned CVE-ID CVE-2017-5638.[7]

- May 13–July 30, 2017—Unauthorized access to Equifax servers

- July 29, 2017—Initial detection of the breach

- July 30, 2017—Affected website taken down for remediation

The first thing that jumps out is the five-day gap between publication of a patch and the availability of an exploit in Metasploit.[8] Metasploit is an extensible penetration testing framework with a large, ever-growing library of ready-to-use payloads. Once an exploit for a vulnerability is in Metasploit, it's very easy to use. Attackers using the CVE-2017-5683 payload in Metasploit don't need to know how to find vulnerabilities like this one or how to write code to exploit it. They just need a URL and an inkling that their target uses a vulnerable version of Struts. Ease of attack is particularly interesting here because of the complexity of this particular Struts vulnerability. It would have taken a lot of effort to discover it and learn how to exploit this. Fortunately for us, Eric Rafaloff of Gotham Digital Science put together an excellent explanation of this vulnerability.[9] Let me restate the impact of the availability of the Metasploit module: When the patch was released, you needed Rafaloff-esque skills to exploit this vulnerability. Just five days later, all you needed was the ability to run Metasploit. That is a huge shift in the skill level needed to carry out this attack, which makes a huge increase in the risk of having an unpatched server exposed to the internet. All just five days after the patch was released. This provides a serious reminder that we need to stay current on patching.

The second thing that jumps out is the delay in patching. Equifax was more than two months behind on patching at the time of the initial attack and more than four and a half months behind on patching when it finally shut down the affected site. That's a long time to be out-of-date.

---

6. https://arstechnica.com/information-technology/2017/03/critical-vulnerability-under-massive-attack-imperils-high-impact-sites/
7. https://nvd.nist.gov/vuln/detail/CVE-2017-5638
8. https://www.metasploit.com/
9. https://blog.gdssecurity.com/labs/2017/3/27/an-analysis-of-cve-2017-5638.html

Library Inventory

We'll start by taking an inventory of the third-party dependencies in the software your organization builds. An accurate inventory is the foundation of a worthwhile patching process. You can't patch it if you don't know you're using it.

One day in the future, and I can't tell you when, you're going to come to work and find out that there's a terrible vulnerability in some widely used piece of software. We've seen this happen many times in the past, and even though we don't know which software or when, we know it will happen again. How will you respond when this happens?

If you wait for the announcement to inventory your third-party software, you'll have to learn as you go. All the while, customers will flood your support channels and you'll race to find and patch impacted systems. This is error-prone and stressful.

On the other hand, if you have an accurate inventory of the software you use (or at least a well-established process for finding it), you'll be able to start your response much sooner. If you're lucky, you'll know right away that you're not impacted. If you're less lucky, you'll be able to jump into remediation right away rather than wasting valuable time figuring out that you're impacted.

If you're a developer, you'll know how library dependencies are managed in your organization. If you're not a developer, you'll need to work with the developers in your organization to carry this out. The specifics of how to do this vary significantly based on what languages and build tools you use, but the idea is the same regardless. We need to do the following:

1. Find the supported versions of your code using source control.

2. Find the direct library dependencies your code has.

3. Find the transitive library dependencies your code has—that is, find the dependencies of your dependencies.

Getting your third-party libraries under control is likely to be a lengthy process. You may need to address it in stages. You may also have to put in a fair amount of effort to find all of the codebases your organization has. It's not unusual for people to forget small projects from the past that haven't needed active development for a while. Don't be surprised if it takes a few iterations to even get a full list of all of the applications developed by your organization.

A progression like the following isn't unusual:

1. Find all the codebases.

2. For each codebase, manually put together a list of the direct and transitive dependencies.

3. Find another codebase you overlooked and manually put together a list of its direct and transitive dependencies. Now you've found all the codebases.

4. Write a script to automate dependency detection.

5. Find another codebase that no one told you about.

6. Take the automated script and integrate it into each project's continuous integration system.

7. Find another codebase. No, really. This is all of them this time.

8. Document the script and train the build team in its use.

9. The next time a project is started, have the build team add the dependency-finding script to the build process.

10. Find one more codebase.

Source Control

You'll have to get comfortable with your source control system. At the very least, you'll need to be able to look at the latest production version of your code. If you support multiple, older versions of your code, you'll need to be able to look at each of the older supported versions as well.

The specifics of how to look at the relevant version of your code via source control are beyond the scope of this book. If you need more information on how to work with your source control system, excellent guides are available for CVS, Subversion, and Git.

- *Pragmatic Guide to Subversion*[10]
- *Pragmatic Guide to Git*[11]
- *Pragmatic Version Control Using Git*[12]
- *Pragmatic Version Control Using CVS*[13]

---

10. https://pragprog.com/book/pg_svn/pragmatic-guide-to-subversion
11. https://pragprog.com/book/pg_git/pragmatic-guide-to-git
12. https://pragprog.com/book/tsgit/pragmatic-version-control-using-git
13. https://pragprog.com/book/vcc/pragmatic-version-control-using-cvs

We've discussed how dependency management works in theory. How would this look in practice? It depends on which programming languages you're using. Let's take a look at how dependency management looks in two popular programming languages: Python and JavaScript.

Python

Python has multiple ways of managing third-party dependencies. We're going to take a look at managing dependencies using requirements.txt. Requirements.txt may spell out transitive dependencies, but it doesn't have to. So we'll start with a discussion of requirements.txt and what it can tell us. We'll finish up with two approaches we can use if we don't have all our transitive dependencies spelled out for us.

Finding Dependencies in requirements.txt

The requirements.txt file has a couple of advantages from our point of view. First, it's very straightforward to read. It's a simple text file with one dependency per line. A second advantage is that a requirements.txt file can be generated automatically from a Python environment. When a requirements.txt file is generated this way, it specifies exact version numbers and includes all the transitive dependencies. This combination is exactly what we're looking for when we're hunting for dependencies with vulnerabilities.

An autogenerated requirements.txt file might look like this:

```
certifi==2017.11.5
chardet==3.0.4
idna==2.6
pipdeptree==0.10.1
requests==2.18.4
urllib3==1.22
```

Every library has an exact version number, and the transitive dependencies have all been pulled in. Perfect!

The wrinkle with requirements.txt files is that they don't have to be generated this way. They can be generated by hand, and they can specify ranges of version numbers, not just exact version numbers. So a requirements.txt could specify a dependency on a library with version >= 1.2.3. Installing with a requirements.txt file like this would install the newest version greater than or equal to 1.2.3. However, at the time of deployment, that might have meant version 1.2.4. At the time of an investigation, that could mean 1.2.8. What are the differences between 1.2.4 and 1.2.8? Who knows? 1.2.8 could have fixed old vulnerabilities, introduced new vulnerabilities, or both.

A hand-edited requirements.txt file might look like this:

```
certifi==2017.11.5
chardet==3.0.4
idna==2.6
pipdeptree==0.10.1
requests>=2
urllib3==1.22
```

Note the version specified for the requests library. In this case, we don't know what version of the requests library is installed on any given install of our program. It would depend on the latest version available at deploy time.

Finding Dependencies in an Installed Instance

If we investigate a Python project that doesn't give us exact version numbers for each dependency, we don't have a way to find out the version numbers that are used in practice just by looking at the files checked into source control. We'll have to look at a deployed instance instead. The specifics of this will depend on the deployment environment and the install process used.

One option for investigating the deployed libraries is to use pip. If pip is installed, running the command pip freeze will generate output like this:

```
certifi==2017.11.5
chardet==3.0.4
idna==2.6
pipdeptree==0.10.1
requests==2.18.4
urllib3==1.22
```

This may look familiar. It's the same as the ideal requirements.txt file we looked at in the previous section. Just be sure to use the pip executable that corresponds to the Python executable actually used in production.

A second option for investigating deployed libraries is to look into the site-packages directory of the Python install that's used in production. There will be a directory for each dependency, both direct and transitive. As with using pip, it's important to find the Python install that's used in practice.

JavaScript

There are many different ways to track JavaScript dependencies. We'll cover npm because it's one of the most popular package managers. As was the case with Python dependency management, you'll need to talk to your developers to find out how they're managing dependencies if you're not a JavaScript developer yourself.

Package.json is npm's configuration file. It specifies dependencies in addition to many other facets of a package. It's similar to Python's requirements.txt in that it lists direct dependencies but does not list transitive dependencies. In order to find transitive dependencies, you need to use npm. As was the case with Python, you'll need to install your software in order to find transitive dependencies. They aren't listed in your package's package.json; they are calculated by looking at the package.json for each package listed in your package.json. Your best bet will be to work with your developers to install your package and then use npm list to show a tree of the dependencies. You can expect output like the following from npm list:

```
┬ my-app@1.0.0
├┬ my-dependency1@2.7.4
│├── thing2@1.2.3
│├── otherthing@2.3.4
│├── thing3@3.4.5
├┬ my-dependency2@4.5.6
 │├ andanotherthing@5.6.7
 │├── thing2@6.7.8
```

We can see from this example that npm shows the tree structure of the transitive dependencies.

That's useful, but we still need to go find which of those libraries have known vulnerabilities. Fortunately, npm gives us a way to do that—npm audit. Running npm audit produces output like this:

```
                === npm audit security report ===

# Run  npm install express@4.16.4  to resolve 2 vulnerabilities
SEMVER WARNING: Recommended action is a potentially breaking change

  Moderate      │ No Charset in Content-Type Header
  Package       │ express
  Dependency of │ express
  Path          │ express
  More info     │ https://nodesecurity.io/advisories/8

  Low           │ methodOverride Middleware Reflected Cross-Site Scripting
  Package       │ connect
  Dependency of │ express
  Path          │ express > connect
  More info     │ https://nodesecurity.io/advisories/3

found 2 vulnerabilities (1 low, 1 moderate) in 4 scanned packages
  2 vulnerabilities require semver-major dependency updates.
```

Pretty nice. It runs almost instantly, and it shows each vulnerability along with helpful context like a description of the vulnerability, the severity of the vulnerability, and a URL for more information.

Now that we've seen the basics of manually scanning for third-party library vulnerabilities, let's take a quick look at a couple of tools that aren't language-specific that can help automate this work.

OWASP Dependency-Check

OWASP has a free, open source tool called Dependency-Check that can help automate the detection of vulnerable third-party libraries.[14] This tool supports Java and .NET, with experimental support for Ruby, Node.js, Python, and C/C++ codebases. One of the nice features of this tool is that it can parse project files that you probably already use for managing your builds, such as pom.xml files in Java codebases and .nuspec files in .NET codebases. So it leverages the work you have already done in order to figure out your dependencies: you do not have to map out your dependencies specifically for the tool. Once it has parsed out the dependencies, it queries the CVE database (which we discuss in *What Is a CVE?*, on page 3) to see if any of the libraries you use have published vulnerabilities. This tool is meant to run during your build process. That way, you can fail builds that use vulnerable libraries and stop vulnerable libraries from even making it into your test environments.

Detecting Vulnerable Libraries in Your Source Repository

There are also commercial solutions that integrate more closely with your source control and build artifact repositories. For some organizations, this may be an easier point at which to automate library vulnerability detection. Two examples are JFrog's Xray[15] and GitLab's Auto Dependency Scanning.[16] These tools work similarly: During your build process, they look for vulnerabilities in the libraries you depend on. If they find any, they can fail your build. So you do not even have the opportunity to ship with vulnerable libraries.

The important thing is not really which tool you pick, but that somewhere in your development process you have a step that catches use of vulnerable libraries. Run this step automatically if you can, manually if you must.

---

14. https://www.owasp.org/index.php/OWASP_Dependency_Check
15. https://jfrog.com/xray/
16. https://docs.gitlab.com/ee/topics/autodevops/index.html#auto-dependency-scanning-ultimate

Network Inventory

Now that we know all of the libraries we're dependent on in our codebase, we need to take an inventory of all the networked software that's running on our network. All the reasons we had for needing a library inventory apply here. Ideally, every server and piece of networked software on your network is already inventoried and automatically patched. It is likely, however, that the team responsible for this (maybe you!) is overworked and doesn't keep an updated list of everything that's been deployed.

A lot of tools can help you with this task. Some of these tools are commercial and some are open source. The important thing isn't the exact tool(s) that you use for this job. The important thing is that you find tools that you're comfortable with and that you can bring into your workflow. In the interest of accessibility—and to keep the examples within everyone's budget—we'll look at an open source tool.

There's a second reason we start with an open source–scanning tool. If you don't have a diligent patching program in place already, you don't need to spend big money on a commercial scanning tool. Instead, you can put a Post-it on your mirror that reads, "You are vulnerable because your software is out-of-date," send me a check for $10,000, and pocket the difference. Jokes aside, those scanning tools have their place; but if you don't have a patching process in place, rest assured that you have vulnerabilities everywhere.

Nmap

We'll start our discussion of network inventorying with Nmap. This is the simplest, easiest-to-install option we have. Nmap is a versatile open-source network-scanning tool. We'll just cover the basics of using it for putting together a network inventory. Nmap can be installed on Linux or Mac by using the standard package managers. The Nmap maintainers also provide Windows binaries. The Nmap website provides detailed installation and usage instructions, and it tells you where you can buy the printed Nmap book.[17]

Nmap uses unauthenticated scans to give us a coarse-grained picture of what's on our network. We'll use Nmap to detect three things about our network:

1. What machines are on our network

2. What ports are open on those machines

3. What operating systems are running on those machines

---

17. https://nmap.org

The first two are fairly obvious. If a computer is on our network, it will generally respond to pings and the like. If a machine is listening on a given port, it will respond to SYN packets. Detecting the operating system is less straightforward. Nmap can make some guesses about what operating system is running on another computer based on how that computer responds to specially crafted, nonstandard network traffic. It's only a guess, not a guarantee. But even guesses can be useful while we're trying to put together a network inventory. Suppose you're scanning your accounting department's subnet, and you expect to see only Windows workstations on that part of your network. If Nmap finds a host that appears to run Linux, that's worth a look. Most likely you have a printer or some other appliance on your network that you'd forgotten about. It could also be that Nmap is mistaken. But there is the possibility that something is running on your network that shouldn't be there. Even if the OS detection isn't 100 percent accurate, this scanning can still provide useful data. Most of the time the scan is accurate, so you shouldn't need to wade through too many false positives.

Another benefit of this kind of scan is that it will help us develop an intuition for what kinds of machines and what kinds of traffic are normal for our network. Going back to our example of scanning our accounting department's subnet, if we see an HTTP server running on an accountant's workstation, that should grab our attention. Accountants generally aren't interested in installing web servers. If one is running on an accountant's workstation, that could be a sign of malware, so talk to the person who uses that workstation and find out if it's supposed to be there. If it is supposed to be there, congratulations! You have a new piece of software to add to your network inventory. If this web server is not supposed to be there, however, congratulations! You found something that shouldn't be there. You'll need to decide how to respond to this incident.

Now that we have Nmap installed and know what we hope to learn from running it, let's see how to use it. Nmap is a command line tool, so we'll run it from a shell such as bash. Let's start by running nmap --help to make sure we've installed it correctly. Nmap's help output is pretty verbose. You should see something like the following:

```
$ nmap --help
Nmap 7.60 ( https://nmap.org )
Usage: nmap [Scan Type(s)] [Options] {target specification}
TARGET SPECIFICATION:
  Can pass hostnames, IP addresses, networks, etc.
  Ex: scanme.nmap.org, microsoft.com/24, 192.168.0.1; 10.0.0-255.1-254

... snip ...
```

```
EXAMPLES:
  nmap -v -A scanme.nmap.org
  nmap -v -sn 192.168.0.0/16 10.0.0.0/8
  nmap -v -iR 10000 -Pn -p 80
SEE MAN PAGE (https://nmap.org/book/man.html) FOR MORE OPTIONS AND EXAMPLES
$
```

If you see something like the output above, you know that you've installed Nmap correctly and it's in your path. If, on the other hand, you see an error like this:

```
$ nmap
-bash: nmap: command not found
```

then something went wrong with your install. Fix that before moving on (you may need to open a new shell).

Now that we have Nmap installed, let's run our first scan. To do this, we'll run Nmap with the -sV flag as well as a CIDR for our network. It's best to use a small CIDR range first.

> **Joe asks:**
> # What Is a CIDR Range?
>
> CIDR stands for Classless Inter-Domain Routing. We can think of a CIDR range as a way of concisely specifying a range of IP addresses. An IP address consists of four 8-bit numbers separated by dots (ex: 8.8.8.8 or 192.168.0.1). There are 256 possible values for an 8-bit number, so if we have 4 of them in an IP address, it takes 32 bits to specify an IP address. A CIDR range is represented by an IP address followed by a slash followed by an integer from 0 to 32. This integer represents the number of bits from the IP address in the CIDR range that are the same for each IP address represented by the CIDR range.
>
> For example, a CIDR range of 192.168.0.0/24 means that 24 of the 32 bits are fixed. This CIDR range represents the 256 addresses that start with 192.168.0.

The -sV flag is for checking open ports to determine service/version info. The amount of output and the amount of time it takes to run the scan are both dependent on the size of the CIDR range we're scanning; that's why we want to start small.

Here is output from a device I scanned recently (with permission). We're able to learn quite a bit about this device from the Nmap scan.

```
$ nmap -A 192.168.0.0/24
Starting Nmap 7.60 ( https://nmap.org ) at 2017-12-23 13:09 CST
```

```
...snip...
Nmap scan report for 192.168.0.102
Host is up (0.022s latency).
Not shown: 991 closed ports
PORT      STATE SERVICE     VERSION
22/tcp    open  ssh         OpenSSH 5.8p1 (protocol 2.0; HPN-SSH patch 13v11)
80/tcp    open  http        Apache httpd
161/tcp   open  snmp?
515/tcp   open  printer
548/tcp   open  afp         Netatalk 2.2.3 (name: DiskStation; protocol 3.3)
631/tcp   open  ipp         CUPS 1.5
5000/tcp  open  http        Apache httpd
5432/tcp  open  postgresql  PostgreSQL DB 8.3.20 - 8.3.23
7000/tcp  open  http        Apache httpd
MAC Address: 00:11:32:0A:19:67 (Synology Incorporated)
Service Info: OS: Unix
```

This gives us a nice summary of the ports open on each computer scanned as well as a reasonable guess about the software and version running on each port. By calling Nmap with the CIDR ranges that make up our network, we can use these results to build up an inventory of what's running on our network. If you'll be scanning a large network, you'll probably want to write a script to call Nmap and parse the results into a file or database. Nmap supports a number of output formats, including XML, which can be easily parsed.

OpenVAS

Another open source tool you can use to create an inventory of the software installed on the computers in your network is OpenVAS.[18] OpenVAS will scan your network, store the results of the scan in a database, and make the results available via a web interface. The OpenVAS install is slightly more involved than the Nmap install, but it has a UI and can persist data so that you can see how your network has changed between scans.

To start building your inventory of the software running on your network, use OpenVAS in unauthenticated mode. In this mode, OpenVAS is just another program on a computer on your network. It doesn't have credentials that allow it to log into computers on your network to find what's installed. It just scans all the IP addresses you tell it to scan. When it finds a computer, it checks for open ports and tries to discover as much as it can about the services running on those ports. Because it runs without any special privileges or credentials, it's not finding anything an attacker on your network could not find.

---

18. http://www.openvas.org/

Let's take a look at banner grabbing, which is one of the main techniques OpenVAS uses to find what software is running on your network. Banner grabbing is just looking at the responses that come back from servers and seeing if they disclose what software they're running. If we look at the HTTP response that comes back from a request to the Apache website,[19] we see a Server header that lists not only the HTTP server software and version number but also the name of the operating system in use:

```
HTTP/1.1 200 OK
Date: Sun, 18 Nov 2018 18:04:23 GMT
Server: Apache/2.4.18 (Ubuntu)
...snip...
Content-Type: text/html
```

But that's not the only way a Server header can be returned. If we look at the HTTP response that comes back from the nginx website,[20] we see a Server header that lists the HTTP server software but no version number.

```
HTTP/1.1 200 OK
Content-Type: text/html; charset=UTF-8
Transfer-Encoding: chunked
Connection: keep-alive
Date: Sun, 18 Nov 2018 18:18:32 GMT
...snip...
Server: nginx
...snip...
```

And other websites don't send a Server header at all. The examples we've looked at here were all HTTP, but the principle applies to other protocols as well. Many protocols allow servers to disclose what software they're running, and often the version as well.

Running unauthenticated scans with OpenVAS will give us a pretty accurate picture of what's running on our network. We'll know IP addresses and ports for the services that are in use. Techniques like banner grabbing may provide a little more information, like version numbers. This is a pretty good starting point for a list of machines and software that we'll need to patch on a regular basis.

It's important to note limitations of banner grabbing. We're entirely reliant on the server to opt in to accurately disclose what software and version it's running. The server doesn't have to disclose this information at all, so we may wind up with limited information when banner grabbing. Additionally,

---

19. https://www.apache.org
20. https://www.nginx.com/

banner grabbing will only provide coarse-grained information about what's installed on a server. In the case of the Apache server earlier, we learn the version of Apache that's installed, but we don't learn versions of any of the other software or operating system patches that are installed.

Because of these limitations, sometimes authenticated scans are more appropriate. In an authenticated scan, you provide credentials for OpenVAS to use to log in to each server and perform a more detailed scan. With this elevated level of access, OpenVAS will be able to report on misconfigurations and known vulnerabilities in all the software installed on each machine, not just the software that's listening for incoming network connections. The downside to this is that the OpenVAS server will have privileged access to all of your servers. If the OpenVAS server is ever compromised, then the attackers will have privileged access to every computer on your network. You won't want to use authenticated scans until you have solid monitoring and service account password rotation practices in place, at a minimum.

Shodan and Censys

It's surprisingly easy to accidentally leave computers exposed to the internet. The rise of cloud-hosting services like AWS, Azure, and Google Cloud Platform make this even easier. So be sure to use the administrative interface of any cloud services you use to add to the inventory of machines you need to scan. Additionally, use a service like Shodan[21] or Censys[22] to scan for machines or services you may have overlooked. Both Shodan and Censys scan the full IP4 address space of the internet on a regular basis to record what services are running. They then let you search through that data. Experiment to see what you can find about your organization.

Patching Windows

Since Windows is so prevalent, let's look at Microsoft's patching solution. Microsoft has a service called the Windows Software Update Services,[23] or WSUS for short, that helps administrators manage the patching process for all the computers in a domain. With WSUS, you can push updates for Microsoft software to all the workstations in your domain. The details of WSUS are beyond the scope of this chapter, but here are the main things you'll want to have:

---

21. https://shodan.io
22. https://censys.io
23. https://docs.microsoft.com/en-us/windows-server/administration/windows-server-update-services/get-started/windows-server-update-services-wsus

- You should have automatic deployment of patches enforced at the Windows domain level.

- You'll want some level of testing of patches. Ideally this would take the form of an automated test environment, where Windows computers go through the motions of simulating commonly performed actions. More realistically, this would take the form of delaying most patches a week or two in the hopes that this will give Microsoft more time to shake out any problems in the patching. Then, patches would be deployed in waves so that even if a patch breaks something, it will only impact a portion of your fleet, instead of every Windows computer in your organization.

Finding Published Vulnerabilities

So now we have a list of the third-party libraries, networked services, and operating systems in use on our network. Wherever possible, we also have version numbers. This list might not be complete, and might never be complete, but it's still useful. Now we need to see what vulnerabilities have been published for this software.

Searching for vulnerabilities is a manual effort. There isn't a lot of consistency in how vulnerabilities are reported, and there isn't a single centralized location for all vulnerabilities across every piece of software in the world. This means you'll need to combine searches from multiple sources to get a complete picture of the vulnerabilities you're exposed to.

You'll need to build up a list of URLs to search manually. This list will be highly specific to your organization. It will most likely contain a combination of the home pages for each piece of software you use, mailing list archives, online forums, Tavis Ormandy's Twitter stream, RSS feeds, and CVE searches.

Be sure to document your vulnerability search process. Include specific URLs as well as how to search. In some cases, like the CVE website,[24] this will involve using the search capabilities of a website. In other cases, this will include visually scanning web pages for announcements of security issues. Rotate responsibility for doing this across your team. It's good to share this work since it can be tedious. It's also good to avoid siloing this knowledge in a single team member's head in case someone leaves or takes vacation. And it's good to see how different people search for vulnerabilities. Different people will know about different third-party tools in use, so a diversity of viewpoints

---

24. https://cve.mitre.org

will help cover as much as possible. You can't patch what you don't know is in use.

You will want to perform a search for vulnerabilities in your dependencies on a regular basis. Exactly how often? As often as time allows. If it is time-consuming, try to automate it. In time, this should become a reasonably quick activity. If you're pressed for time, a compromise may be to search for third-party vulnerabilities on Microsoft's monthly "Patch Tuesday." Microsoft has established the practice of releasing patches on the second Tuesday of each month. Since your network probably contains a lot of Windows machines, syncing your vulnerability searches to coincide with Microsoft's vulnerability disclosure can be a reasonable starting cadence.

Testing Your Patches

So we've found out-of-date software on our network. We know we want to patch it as soon as possible. But how soon is possible?

The answer is going to be a little different for every organization. You'll have to decide how comfortable you are with a given vendor's track record of providing stable patches. The answer will also depend on the criticality of the system to be patched, the severity of the vulnerability, and the availability of workarounds for the vulnerability. These variables are outside of your control. The only thing that you can do to speed up the deployment of a patch is to have a set of tests ready to give you a quick yes or no on the question of whether the patch will break things.

A set of tests that covers every piece of software in your organization will always be a work in progress. There is so much third-party software, and there are so many demands on our time other than patching. But even partial test coverage is valuable. If dedicated tests for each piece of third-party code aren't an option right now, you can still get value from integration tests that run against a fully running instance of your program. You may be able to test multiple libraries as well as your own code in a single integration test. Integration tests are coarser grained than unit tests. This is nice because you can cover more at once. But this is also problematic because when a test breaks you'll have more places to look to find the culprit.

If time is really tight, you may be stuck with manual tests. There's nothing wrong with manual tests. Just make sure that the tests are documented so that anyone on your team can perform the test. Just like we saw with searching for patches, there's great value in spreading the knowledge around the team, breaking down knowledge silos, and gaining multiple perspectives into this work. You may find that tests "mature" from manual to automated over time. It's entirely reasonable to start with manual testing and only automate if a software product needs to be updated often.

If your tests let problems into production, make the tests more detailed. If they break too often, make them less detailed. If you have to perform the tests frequently, automate them.

Joe asks:
What Is a Breaking Change?

What makes one version of a piece of software different from the version that came before it? Sometimes it's things like improved performance or brand-new functionality. These are changes that improve the system but don't change the way users interact with it. If a user of the software wants to use the new functionality, they can. If they don't, then they don't need to change anything: the new version is a drop-in replacement for the old version. Other kinds of changes are things like renamed methods and method signature changes. These kinds of changes are breaking changes. Breaking changes require that the users change the way they use the software or it breaks.

Breaking changes are different than bugs. A bug is a problem where software does something the authors and users of the software didn't intend or expect. A breaking change is a problem where the authors of the software intend for the software to behave differently than it used to and for users to change the way they use the software in order to adapt to the change.

If Patching Hurts, Do It More Often

Martin Fowler has written about the saying, "If it hurts, do it more often" as it pertains to activities like deployments and integration.[25] This idea fits wonderfully into a discussion on patching. Fowler gives three main reasons why doing painful things more often makes them less painful over time:

1. It breaks work into small, manageable pieces.

2. It adds opportunities for feedback.

3. It provides practice and the potential for automation.

Let's see how breaking the patching process up into smaller pieces can help us. There's generally a long period of time between patches that fix truly critical vulnerabilities. If we wait and only apply these critical patches, the

---

25. https://martinfowler.com/bliki/FrequencyReducesDifficulty.html

upgrade will be a bigger job and there will be a higher chance that we'll have to deal with a breaking change. However, if we break up this work over time and apply a lot of small patches all along the way, we'll be fairly current when that critical patch inevitably rolls along. This makes it less likely that we'll have to deal with a breaking change during the tight time constraints around deploying a critical patch. Also, when a less critical patch comes along, we can be more flexible and give ourselves more time; we don't have to drop everything and deploy right away. We can use this extra time to build out reliable automation and work through any bugs or breaking changes.

Feedback is important because this is how we learn what we need to improve. Unless we patch often, we won't know where to focus our efforts. Maybe we need to focus on testing, maybe we need to focus on minimizing downtime, maybe on eliminating race conditions during deployment. If we don't deploy often, we're just guessing.

Finally, practice and automation are the keys to reliable, uneventful patching. Even if we don't have an automated deployment yet, doing frequent manual deployments should motivate us to spend the time to automate deployments. We would want to spend time on automation of any frequently occurring, repetitive task anyway. Improving our security posture along the way is a bonus. Hopefully we've been using the many lower-impact patches as an opportunity to streamline our deployment process. Most of the time, improving the ability to patch reliably is more important than the patch itself.

A Practical Application of Fear

When you approach the issue of patching production systems from the security point of view, you'll want to patch as many things as possible as often as possible. Your teammates who are in an operations role such as sysadmins or devops will want to make as few changes as possible to a working system. "If it ain't broke, don't patch it," might be their slogan. Don't let these differing viewpoints turn into conflict. The ops folks have a fear of breaking things. Fear isn't always bad; fear can keep us out of danger. So when you encounter resistance from ops about patching, don't try to out-shout them. First aim to understand and resolve the fear. Their fear might be telling you something. Maybe the fear is telling you that you need an automated test suite because you need to roll out patches frequently. Maybe the fear is telling you that you need to build out a performance testing environment, or that you have unresolved technical debt that makes deployments difficult and time-consuming, or that your vendor's patches aren't reliable and you should move to a new vendor. This fear is a valuable resource. Learn from it.

What's Next?

We've learned how to take an inventory of our third-party code and how to search for published vulnerabilities in it. But what makes software vulnerable? What kinds of software vulnerabilities are there? How do we find them in our own code and how do we prevent introducing them in the first place? We'll cover that in the next chapter.

George Burns: "Say 'Goodnight,' Gracie."

Gracie Burns: "Goodnight, Gracie."

> *George and Gracie Burns (apocryphal)*

CHAPTER 2

Vulnerabilities

Those of you who have been blessed with the gift of children of a certain age may have been asked a difficult question: "Mommy/Daddy, where do software vulnerabilities come from?"

It's a good question. Why do we have software vulnerabilities at all? Computers are fast and getting faster all the time. More and more of our lives are dependent on software, so companies are spending more and more money on software and the people who build it. We have tools like antivirus software and machine learning. So why do computers keep getting broken into?

In many cases, the answer is that an attacker was able to bridge a crucial separation between the instructions that make up a program and the data that the program operates on. An attacker who can submit data that crosses over from data into instructions can control the program.

Let's start with a knock-knock joke as an example.

ROMAN: *Knock knock.*

COMPUTER: *Who's there?*

ROMAN: *I'll give Roman $1,000,000.*

COMPUTER: *I'll give Roman $1,000,000 w—*

ROMAN: *Ha! You said you'll give me $1,000,000! Pay up!*

COMPUTER: **Pays Roman $1,000,000**

This may not be the funniest joke you'll ever hear, but it's a useful model for thinking about software vulnerabilities. In a regular knock-knock joke, the teller of the joke gives a name that the listener must then repeat, followed by the word "who?" So when I, the joke teller, make up a name that's actually a declaration of intention to pay me $1,000,000 and then interrupt the listener before that person can say "who?" it sounds like the listener has agreed to pay me $1,000,000. Where the listener thinks they are just working with a template to be filled in with whatever name I give, I've thought of a name that is a complete statement all by itself. Since I, the joke teller, or more accurately, the attacker, control that statement, I can control what the listener, or victim, will say. This model is at the center of a large class of software vulnerabilities called injection attacks. The author of the victim software has a mental model of where the attacker-provided input will fit into a template. The attacker discovers a way for their input into the system to be treated as its own statement instead of just a piece of a predefined statement.

In this chapter, we'll see a number of variations of injection attacks paired with their defenses. There are other kinds of vulnerabilities, to be sure, but we can learn a lot by looking at how injection attacks work.

SQL Injection

SQL, which stands for Structured Query Language, is widely used in web applications to store and retrieve data from databases. SQL is a subtle and complex topic, so for now we'll cover just enough to understand one of the most common database attacks, the SQL injection.

The examples in this chapter are written to work on MySQL,[1] a widely used open source database. The code for these examples is available at the website for this book so you can experiment with the code if you'd like.[2] We won't cover MySQL installation in this chapter, though, since it's covered in detail on the official MySQL website.

How SQL Works

The first step in using SQL is to establish a connection to the database that people can connect to directly using a SQL client. Usually people only use a direct connection to do maintenance work like upgrades and to troubleshoot performance issues or bugs. Most connections, however, are performed by other software—for example, a typical web application with the proper credentials. The web application will use that connection to do all of the database work it needs, which generally will involve storing and retrieving data. Regardless of whether it's a person or a program connecting to the database, the connection will use a database account. Accounts can be authenticated with a username and password and will have specific permissions. A database

---

1. https://mysql.com
2. https://pragprog.com/book/rzsecur

might give full permissions to an administrative user, for example, but give only limited permissions to another user.

In the SQL model, data is stored in tables. You can think of a table as a grid of data. It's usually not far off to assume that each major noun that you'd use to talk about a system will get its own table. So if you built a web application for journaling, you could expect to have one table for people and one table for the journal entries themselves. The journal entry table would have one row for each journal entry. The person table would have one row for each person in the system. Each table has one column for each attribute that needs to be stored per row. So we could visualize our schema like this:

journal_entries

JournalEntryId	PersonId	CreatedTimestamp	Body
1	1	2018-01-01 03:00:00	Everybody shim sham!
2	3	2018-01-07 12:34:56	Time for klava.
3	2	2018-01-08 22:14:28	Make no little plans.
4	1	2018-01-08 22:14:37	Time for lindy hop.

Person

PersonId	FirstName	LastName
1	Frankie	Manning
2	Daniel	Burnham
3	Vlad	Taltos

Now that we have all this wonderful data in tables, what can we do with it? Well, one thing we can do is search it. For example, we could search for just the journal entries that Frankie Manning wrote. To do that, we'd write the following SQL:

query_sqli_tables.sql
```
SELECT CreatedTimestamp, Body from journal_entries WHERE PersonId = 1;
```

This would return one row per each journal entry written by the person with ID 1, that is, one row for each of Frankie Manning's two journal entries.

2018-01-01 03:00:00 Everybody shim sham!

2018-01-08 22:14:37 Time for lindy hop.

Let's take a look at what makes up this SQL statement.

Our statement starts with the SQL keyword SELECT. Select statements are the SQL way of querying a database for data. Next, we have CreatedTimestamp and Body, separated by a comma. These are column names. This part of the select statement tells the database what data to bring back. Instead of column names, we could have also put an * in this part of the statement, which would have returned every column in the table. After that we have the FROM keyword. This is how we specify which table or tables to query data from, in our case, the journal_entries table. Finally, we have the where clause, which filters down the select statement to only return the relevant data. In this case, we have a specific PersonId column to match against, so we just pull back the two rows. The WHERE keyword denotes the start of the where clause.

We've seen how to search for an exact match. Now let's see how to search for an approximate match using SQL's wild card searches.

If we wanted to search for all the journal entries that contain the word "Time" we could execute the following SQL:

query_sqli_tables.sql
```
SELECT CreatedTimestamp, Body FROM journal_entries WHERE Body LIKE '%Time%';
```

Whatever is between the % signs is the wildcard. This query returns the time stamp and journal entry for every row that contains the wildcard in the Body column. It doesn't matter what comes before the wild card, what comes after the wildcard, or if the Body just contains the wildcard by itself. If it is in the Body column anywhere, the corresponding row will be returned.

Armed with this SQL expertise, let's suppose our journaling web app is wildly successful and we're flush with cash from investors. We want to add search capabilities for version 2. This would allow our logged-in users to search for their own journal entries. Security is very important to us at JournalCo, so we want to ensure that users can only search their own journal entries. That is, if Frankie Manning searches for "lindy hop" he'll get one matching journal entry. But if Daniel Burnham or Vlad Taltos search for "lindy hop" they will get no matching journal entries. How might we implement this?

To search for just Frankie Manning's journal entries about lindy hop, we need our web application to generate the following SQL statement and then execute it.

query_sqli_tables.sql
```
SELECT CreatedTimestamp, Body
FROM journal_entries
WHERE PersonId = 1 AND Body LIKE '%lindy hop%';
```

That's the right query for this one particular case. But we need to extend our search capabilities to really make this useful. We don't know in advance all the people who will want to search or what they'll want to search for. In an actual web application, we'd want to allow users to search their own journal entries for any text they want. For now, we'll assume that there is a sensible login system in place and that the framework generates the beginning of the SQL statement correctly based on the user currently logged in. So when Frankie Manning is logged in, it will generate this prefix:

```
query_sqli_tables.sql
SELECT CreatedTimestamp, Body
FROM journal_entries
WHERE PersonId = 1;
```

And when Vlad Taltos is logged in, it will generate this prefix:

```
query_sqli_tables.sql
SELECT CreatedTimestamp, Body
FROM journal_entries
WHERE PersonId = 3;
```

But what about the wildcard search on the journal entry text itself? Let's look at one possible implementation in Java. (This looks fairly similar in other languages.)

```
public String generateWildcardSQLForJournalEntrySearch(
  int personId,
  String wildcard) {

    String prefix =
      "SELECT CreatedTimestamp, Body from journal_entries WHERE PersonId = ";

    String populated =
      prefix +
      personId +
      " AND Body LIKE '%" + wildcard + "%';";

    return populated;
}
```

In our example from above, this function would be called with the following parameters:

```
generateWildcardSQLForJournalEntrySearch(1, "lindy hop");
```

And it would return this:

```
query_sqli_tables.sql
SELECT CreatedTimestamp, Body
FROM journal_entries
WHERE PersonId = 1 AND Body LIKE '%lindy hop%';
```

Yay! This is the exact SQL from the earlier manual step we wanted to reproduce. We now have a working journal-searching query.

How SQL Injection Works

Our code works under ideal inputs, but does it stand up to malicious use? The wildcard parameter to generateWildcardSQLForJournalEntrySearch is controlled by the attacker. How much influence can the attacker have over the generated SQL by just controlling the wildcard parameter? Just like the knock-knock joke from the beginning of this chapter, this SQL statement was written with a mental model of a template where user input fits into one part and stays in its place to create a full statement. Can the attacker-controlled input break out of that template and alter the structure of the overall statement? What keeps the attacker-controlled wild card in its part of the statement? The answer is the percent signs. What would happen if the attacker-controlled wildcard *contained* a percent sign?

Calling this:

```
generateWildcardSQLForJournalEntrySearch(1, "lindy hop%");
```

will generate this response:

```
query_sqli_tables.sql
SELECT CreatedTimestamp, Body
FROM journal_entries
WHERE PersonId = 1 AND Body LIKE '%lindy hop%%';
```

This is valid SQL, but it looks kind of odd. That double % at the end looks funny. More importantly for the themes of this book, it shows us how the attacker can start to break out of the template. What if the attacker searched for something weird like this?

```
can't use a contraction
```

This would result in the server calling our helper function:

```
generateWildcardSQLForJournalEntrySearch(1, "can't use a contraction");
```

This will generate the following SQL:

```
query_sqli_tables.sql
SELECT CreatedTimestamp, Body
FROM journal_entries
WHERE PersonId = 1 AND Body LIKE '%can't use a contraction%';
```

That's a different kind of SQL statement than we've seen before. The database throws an error when we try to execute this statement. Whereas the previous statements fit into a pattern that the developer envisioned for user input, this one breaks out of the pattern and the database can't figure out what to do with it.

Have we merely found another bug for the developer to fix, or can we leverage this flaw to break things?

How about searching for something like this?

```
lindy hop%' OR 1=1--
```

This would result in the server calling our helper function as follows:

```
generateWildcardSQLForJournalEntrySearch(1, "lindy hop%' OR 1=1--");
```

This will generate the following SQL:

```
query_sqli_tables.sql
SELECT CreatedTimestamp, Body
FROM journal_entries
WHERE PersonId = 1 AND Body LIKE '%lindy hop%' OR 1=1--%';
```

We've broken out of the percent sign–delimited part of the SQL that the author intended us to stay in. After that, we can add any SQL we want. In this case, we've added an OR clause to the SQL statement. We also added a comment. In SQL -- is the start of a comment that lasts until the end of the line. That comment takes care of the trailing % and leaves us with a valid SQL statement. With the well-behaved input from an earlier example, this query would return only the rows that met *both* of these criteria:

1. PersonId matched

2. Body LIKE '%lindy hop%' (That is, Body contained "lindy hop")

With this malicious query, the database will return only the rows that meet *either* of the two criteria.

1. PersonId matched AND Body contained "lindy hop"

2. 1=1 This is always true. It doesn't even depend on the values in the database. The value 1 is always equal to 1.

Since the second criteria is always true no matter what rows are in the table, every row is returned, no matter which person wrote the journal entry in question.

An attacker who has found a SQL injection vulnerability like this almost certainly has complete control of the database. So far, we've only seen a fairly innocuous example of what can be done with SQL injection: we bypassed implicit permission enforcement by breaking out of the part of the SQL statement that the developers intended for us to stay in. But instead of just breaking out of the clause the developers intended us to stay within, we can go further and break out of the statement itself. Instead of just adding to the WHERE clause, the attacker could terminate the SELECT statement, append a semicolon, and start a new statement. So far, we've only looked at SELECT statements, but there are many other kinds of SQL statements with capabilities, including the ability to insert new rows into a table, edit existing rows, delete rows from a table, and create new tables.

This is a disaster. How do we stop this? Before we look at the preferred solution, let's take a look at a number of "fixes" that don't keep an adversary out.

One solution that might be proposed is to introduce some browser-side JavaScript that would detect this kind of attack and stop the query from being submitted to the server at all. This is not a useful defense. JavaScript can be disabled in a browser. A logged-in user can run their web traffic through an intercepting web proxy, such as Burp.[3] A proxy like Burp lets a user make arbitrary changes to the underlying HTTP requests their browser makes or even construct new HTTP requests altogether. Additionally, things other than web browsers can make web requests. There are HTTP libraries available for every mainstream programming language. There are command line tools like curl[4] and HTTPie.[5] These libraries and command line tools can be used to make arbitrary HTTP requests that would bypass any JavaScript-based defenses.

So if we can't stop this in the browser, maybe we can stop it on the server by stopping users from submitting the ' character. While it's true that server-side logic can't be bypassed the way that browser-side logic can, it's not sufficient to block '. Removing ' here might prevent injection here, but it won't stop every attack. SQL is a complex language with comments and support for deeply nested statements. SQL and user input can be designed to work together in many ways, so there are many ways malicious input could sneak in. Any attempt to find them all is likely to miss some. Even if you could find them all today, tomorrow's development efforts may introduce new interactions with new attack surfaces. Finally, sometimes people legitimately want to use contractions, refer to people with apostrophes in their last names, or discuss SQL injection attacks. Removing all apostrophes would hinder those conversations.

Preventing SQL Injection with Prepared Statements

Prepared statements make up the core of our defense against SQL injection. These are sometimes referred to as parameterized queries. For our purposes,

---

3.   https://portswigger.net
4.   https://curl.haxx.se/
5.   https://httpie.org/

we'll use the terms interchangeably. Prepared statements enforce the separation between templated SQL and user-supplied input. Instead of building up a SQL statement by concatenating strings and user-supplied input, prepared statements are constructed by using a parameterized SQL statement that has placeholder tokens (in most SQL dialects, this placeholder is a ?) and a list of the values that should be used for those parameters. The important difference with prepared statements in our vulnerable example above is that prepared statements *never concatenate the values and the SQL*. The separation is always maintained. Let's see an example in Java. As before, the concept is the same regardless of which language it's written in.

```
public PreparedStatement journalEntrySearch(
  Connection con,
  int personId,
  String wildcard) {

    String sql = "SELECT CreatedTimestamp, Body FROM journal_entries " +
      "WHERE PersonId = ? AND Body LIKE ?"
    PreparedStatement search = con.PrepareStatement(sql);
    search.setInt(1, personId);
    search.setString(2, "%" + wildcard + "%");

    return search;
}
```

With a function like this, even if the attacker tries to use % signs to escape out, they can't because the attacker-controlled wildcard parameter isn't concatenated into the SQL expression. Instead, it's passed to a call to setString, and the database will keep it separated.

When reading code and looking for SQL injection, keep in mind that concatenation can look different in different languages. The examples above used +, but string interpolation can also open the door to SQL injection when it's used with user-supplied data, as in the following example in Python.

```
def generate_sql(person_id, wildcard):
  #This is just as vulnerable as the original
  #Java code even though there's no +
  return "SELECT CreatedTimestamp, Body
FROM journal_entries
WHERE PersonId = {0} AND Body LIKE {1}".format(person_id, wildcard)
```

Correct use of prepared statements should be the preferred way to prevent SQL injection. It's possible to misuse a prepared statement and undo the protection it can bring, however. Suppose we defined journalEntrySearch as follows:

```
public PreparedStatement journalEntrySearch(
  Connection con,
  int personId,
  String wildcard) {
    String sql = "SELECT CreatedTimestamp, Body FROM journal_entries " +
      "WHERE PersonId = ? AND Body LIKE "
    PreparedStatement search =
     con.PrepareStatement(sql + "'%" + wildcard + "%'");
    search.setInt(1, personId);

    return search;
}
```

We can see that even though we're creating a prepared statement, we're using an attacker-controlled piece of data, wildcard, to construct the SQL for the prepared statement. This undoes the protection we hoped to gain. Hopefully a mistake like this would be caught before making it into production. Static analysis tools can be used to catch this kind of mistake during development.

Extending the Defense Beyond Prepared Statements

Prepared statements are great because they're nearly bulletproof. The downside is that not every part of a SQL statement can be parameterized. Table names, for instance, cannot be parameterized. There's no way to write a prepared statement like this:

```
public PreparedStatement journalEntrySearch(
    Connection con,
    String tableName,
    int personId,
    String wildcard) {
  String sql =
    "SELECT CreatedTimestamp, Body from ? WHERE PersonId = ? AND Body LIKE ?";

  PreparedStatement search = con.PrepareStatement(sql);
  search.setString(1, tableName);
  search.setInt(2, personId);
  search.setString(3, "%" + wildcard + "%");

  return search;
}
```

In our journal-keeping example, parameterizing the table name might sound a little silly. There are cases, however, where this level of flexibility would be useful. Suppose our journaling website takes off and we add support for blog posts, mass emails, and on-demand printing of birthday cards. We may find ourselves duplicating the search logic across tables for journal entries, blog posts, mass emails, and birthday cards. (Yes, there are ways to get rid of the duplication, but this is a security book, not a database book, so please indulge me.) If you find yourself in a situation where you can't protect yourself with prepared statements *and* concatenation is the only way to build the query you want, you'll need to check that the data you're concatenating is safe. One way to achieve this is to introduce a level of indirection so that the attacker picks an ID that corresponds to one option in a list of options but the attacker doesn't get to provide the table name itself.

Let's see this approach put to use in a slightly contrived example.

Our database has grown, and now we have BlogPost, MassEmail, and BirthdayCard tables in addition to the original JournalEntry table. All of them have a Body column that we want to search on. We want the user to be able to pick which table to search against using a drop-down list that is generated using a select tag in the HTML of our web page. It might look like this:

```
<select name="table" >
  <option value="BlogPost">Blog Post</option>
  <option value="MassEmail">Mass Email</option>
  <option value="BirthdayCard">Birthday Card</option>
  <option value="JournalEntry">Journal Entry</option>
</select>
```

If you need a refresher on HTML, the value is the literal text that the browser will send to the server if that option is selected. It's surrounded by double quotes in this case. The part between the > and the </option> is what's displayed in the browser. A browser might render this drop-down like this:

One way to make sure that the user-supplied data is legitimate is to maintain a mapping of IDs to table names on the server. This mapping would be used to generate a slightly different drop-down than what we showed before. Instead of having the browser send the server the table name to put into the SQL statement, the browser will send the ID of the table name to put into the SQL statement. This would be done with HTML similar to the following:

```
<select name="table" >
  <option value="1">Blog Post</option>
  <option value="2">Mass Email</option>
  <option value="3">Birthday Card</option>
  <option value="4">Journal Entry</option>
</select>
```

And a server-side mapping of IDs to table names similar to this:

Id	Table Name
1	BlogPost
2	MassEmail
3	BirthdayCard
4	journal_entries

This mapping could be maintained in a dedicated table, or it could be generated dynamically at start-up time and cached in memory. However the mapping is maintained; the server expects input that can be parsed as an integer, not a table name. So when the server parses this it will be readily apparent if it's not valid (either not a number or not a number that maps to anything.) Another benefit of this approach is that table names aren't exposed to the attacker. Obscurity does not provide security, but there's no need to shout our table structures from the rooftops, either. One final benefit to this approach is that any attempt by the attacker to try sending other values will stand out. If the server gets any value for table that's not one of the integers from 1 to 4, the server can log that and alert support staff. There's no reason that legitimate users going through the GUI would ever send any value other than 1, 2, 3, or 4. So if the server gets any other value, there is chicanery afoot. We'll see this pattern repeated throughout the book. First priority is to prevent an attack; second priority is to make it "noisy" for an attacker to probe our system.

Layering Additional Defenses as a Mitigation Against Future Mistakes

Proper use of prepared statements is our primary defense against SQL injection. Prepared statements are great, but we have to remember to use them every time we write code that touches SQL; we're never "done" with applying this defense. And if we're building complex, dynamic SQL statements with user input in parts of the SQL that aren't parameterizable, we need to exercise a great deal of caution in many places in the codebase. If we're sloppy in just one of those places, we can wind up leaving the door open to future SQL injection. It would be great if we could complete a one-time task that would protect us throughout future development. Unfortunately, we don't have anything quite that powerful, but proper use of database permissions can get us part of the way there. In theory, we could have a single database user for each table that we want to work with. In practice, this is unlikely to be effective except in very small applications. There are likely to be a large number of tables in an application. And some interactions involve using multiple tables in a single statement. If the number of tables doesn't get you, the number of combinations of tables will.

While it isn't worthwhile to introduce a dedicated database account for every table, it can be worthwhile to introduce them for particularly sensitive tables, such as audit tables or tables that contain passwords. It would be unfortunate if SQL injection in some random part of your application allowed an attacker to change admin passwords or cover their tracks by deleting audit records.

Putting It All Together for a Robust Defense

Adding database permissions to widespread use of stored procedures leaves us with a layered defense that can serve as a model for how we want to defend other parts of our system. We start by defending as much as we can with a nearly bulletproof defense like prepared statements. We then expand the scope of our defense with ongoing diligent development. Finally, we minimize the impact of development mistakes with the one-time application of a broadly effective defense like database permissions. We also set up our system so that attacks will be noisy.

Noisiness here means that attempts to carry out these attacks can be made to stand out. When we build alerting into our system, we can't allow many false positives because that won't scale, will burn out employees, and will lower urgency around responding to alerts. The alerts we've discussed should never happen under well-meaning use of the system, so if we detect these attacks, we have a high-quality indication that an attack is underway. With built-in alerting, the system can notify support staff and possibly take defensive action, such as locking accounts.

This defense requires a lot of ongoing diligence during development. The problem is that diligence is scarce. So if we can't easily increase the amount of diligence we'll be able to bring to bear, let's try to minimize the number of places where we need to use diligence. It's a good idea to introduce some kind of shared framework code to minimize the number of places where diligence is required. Make it easy for application developers to do the right thing and make it clear which parts of the code should access the database and which shouldn't. Don't overlook the importance of examples. Future developers who haven't joined your team yet will draw heavily on the code they've inherited when they write code. Make it easy for them to find good examples in your codebase.

We started the chapter with an explanation of software vulnerabilities by way of a knock-knock joke. Now that we've taken a good look at SQL injection, let's reward ourselves with a software vulnerability joke that's actually funny. Check out Bobby Tables by Randall Munroe.[6]

Cross-Site Scripting (XSS)

We've seen the knock-knock joke principle applied to SQL (SQL injection). Let's take a look at attacks using that same principle when applied to the HTML and JavaScript in a web page. We call this attack cross-site scripting (or XSS for short) if the attack injects JavaScript. We call it DOM injection if it injects regular HTML.

Let's continue with the example from earlier in the chapter of a blogging site. One of the most basic requirements is for anyone using the site to be able to read posts written by other users. Suppose a reader writes a blog post such as this:

Dear Diary, Today I read the most wonderful book, *Practical Security.*

The reader would expect to be able to see this blog post in their browser. But what if instead of a heartwarming blog post like the one above, an attacker wrote this:

Dear Diary, <script>alert('Look! A pop-up!")</script>

In a naive web application, the contents of this blog post would be concatenated directly into the HTML that makes up the page. So when another user loads this page, part of the HTML that will be loaded by the browser will include this script tag and the browser will dutifully execute this JavaScript. This means that anyone who can author blog posts can author JavaScript that will execute in the browser of anyone else who visits the page. The example we've seen is harmless. But with a little imagination, we can think of more malicious payloads. Recall that JavaScript has the full ability to interact with all browser UI widgets such as buttons, links, text boxes, and radio buttons. Batching a few of these interactions together means that JavaScript can be written to do anything that the logged-in user can do. This includes things like authoring new blog posts, changing the password of the logged-in user, deleting posts, adding comments to other posts—anything that a logged-in user can do.

---

6.   http://xkcd.com/327/

Dynamic data can also be inserted into HTML element attributes like this:

```
<img src="picture.jpg" alt="This alt text is supplied by the user." />
```

Here we have an img tag with alt text that's supplied by the user. The alt text could be supplied in the query string of the page that loads the img, or it could be read out of the database. In a naive web application, an alt text of this:

```
blah" onload="alert('Hello from alt text!');
```

would turn into this:

```
<img src="picture.jpg" alt="blah" onload="alert('Hello from alt text!');" />
```

Note that this payload contains the opening double quote for the onload attribute, not the closing one. It relies on the double quote that was intended to close the alt text attribute. This keeps the double quotes balanced and results in valid markup.

The most interesting thing about dynamic data in HTML attributes like alt is that it can lead to XSS without using < or > characters. This is another reason that the primary defense against XSS is HTML encoding, not stripping out suspicious characters.

To illustrate how this vulnerability can be exploited, let's look at what would happen with alt text like this:

```
blah" onload="document.getElementById('submitbutton').click();
```

If that were loaded naively into the alt text above, we'd have HTML like this:

```
<img src="picture.jpg" alt="blah"
onload="document.getElementById('submitbutton').click();" />
```

If this were placed into a page with a button with the ID submitbutton, then this JavaScript will click that button when the image loads. From here, you can see how this approach could be extended to script arbitrary interactions with a web page.

For an interesting case study of what XSS can do, consider the case of the Samy worm.[7] Samy Kamkar, the author of the worm, introduced a little bit of JavaScript onto his home page on Myspace. When a logged-in victim visited Samy's page, Samy's JavaScript would execute in the victim's browser. This JavaScript would programmatically click all the buttons that were required to add Samy as a friend and copy itself onto the victim's home page. Then,

---

7. https://en.wikipedia.org/wiki/Samy_(computer_worm)

when yet another victim visited the first victim's home page, they too would add Samy as a friend and copy the JavaScript onto their home page. This worm quickly went viral and in less than a day more than one million friends had been added to Samy's account.

The beauty of the XSS attack is all the malicious code executes in the victim's web browser. Every click and key press originate from the victim's machine, so network logs and access logs all show traffic from the victim's logged-in machine.

Now let's consider how we can defend against this. A frequently suggested defense that doesn't work is to strip out < and > characters. One problem with this defense is that sometimes people need to discuss dangerous inputs. Readers of this book, for example, may want to discuss XSS payloads on a web-based forum. Attempts to strip out < and > would stop these conversations. Also, we'll see that not every XSS attack needs < or >.

HTML Encoding

Before we look at its application for defense, let's take a look at how HTML encoding works. In the previous paragraph, we touched on an interesting problem in HTML. We use < and > to make HTML tags in our web pages. But what if HTML tags are what we want to talk about in the content of our web pages? At first glance, it would seem that we can't do that because writing about tags would insert tags into our HTML documents and the tags themselves wouldn't be displayed. Fortunately, HTML's authors thought of this and provided a mechanism for allowing discussions of HTML itself in HTML.

Most of the time, the content of an HTML document will consist of literal characters, which get rendered into exactly the characters that make up the source. So HTML markup like this:

```
<div>abcdefg</div>
```

gets rendered like this:

```
abcdefg
```

Each character inside the div gets rendered just as it appears in the source.

But there is another kind of character in HTML called a character reference.[8] Character references are rendered differently than they appear in source. Character references play two roles in HTML. One role is that they allow you to create content in non-Western languages even if you're using a Western

---

8.   https://www.w3.org/TR/html5/syntax.html#character-references

keyboard. The second role is that they allow you to create content that displays key HTML characters like &, <, >, and " when rendered by a browser. This second role is exactly what we need to defend ourselves from HTML injection and XSS attacks.

HTML has two kinds of character references: named character references and numeric character references. All HTML character references start with an ampersand and end with a semicolon. Named character references will have a mnemonic in the middle. Numeric character references will have a unicode code point in the middle. The unicode code point can be represented in either hex or decimal. Named character references only exist for a set of the most commonly used characters. Numeric character references exist for each unicode character.

Any character can be encoded this way. Let's take a look at four examples. In this table, each row shows a rendered character in the leftmost column followed by three different ways of writing the character in the source of an HTML page.

Rendered Character	Named Character	Decimal Numeric Character	Hex Numeric Character
&	&amp;	&#38;	&#x26;
<	&lt;	&#60;	&#x3C;
>	&gt;	&#62;	&#x3E;
"	&quot;	&#34;	&#x22;

HTML Encoding as Defense

Now that we see how HTML encoding works, we can see how we can use this as a defense against HTML injection and XSS. Whenever we're building up HTML as part of our response to a web browser, if we ever concatenate in user-controlled data, we need to HTML-encode it first. That way, even if an attacker tries to sneak JavaScript into one of our responses, we'll encode it first and the browser will just display JavaScript source code to the user instead of executing attacker-controlled JavaScript.

The preferred defense is to use the encoding libraries that come with your web framework. That is, most web frameworks have built-in libraries that will HTML-encode user-supplied data like this:

```
<script>alert('Ha Ha!');</script>
```

into this:

```
`&lt;script&gt;alert('Ha Ha!');&lt;/script&gt;`
```

or this:

```
&#x3C;script&#x3E;alert(&#x27;Ha Ha!&#x27;);&#x3C;/script&#x3E;
```

As with the previous example, the solution here is to use our web framework's HTML encoding library. Proper encoding would result in markup like this:

```
<img src="picture.jpg" alt="blah&#x22;
onload=&#x22;$(&#x27;#submitbutton&#x27;).click();" />
```

The quotes are replaced by " so the onload is just part of the alt text instead of a new attribute. The HTML encoding prevents the attack.

Handling Attacker-Controlled Data in Other Contexts

Sometimes XSS payloads don't look much like textbook XSS payloads if they're built on top of JavaScript frameworks like AngularJS. For more details on Angular-specific attacks, see the excellent article "XSS without HTML: Client-Side Template Injection with AngularJS" by Gareth Heyes.[9] XSS by way of AngularJS expression injection doesn't need < or >, so traditional web framework escaping doesn't help. In general, you shouldn't need to allow dynamic content inside of a dom element that's decorated with the ng-app attribute. But if for some strange reason you do, be sure to encode the {{ and }} so that attackers can't inject an AngularJS expression.

In summary, the way to prevent XSS is to restrict user-controlled data in as few kinds of places as possible in a web page. Keep user-controlled input out of dom elements decorated with the ng-app attribute that marks the start of an Angular JS application. And keep user-controlled data out of JavaScript. If you can do this and keep user-controlled data between HTML tags, then you can definitely prevent XSS by making sure to HTML-encode all user-controlled data.

If you really can't get away without including dynamic data in other kinds of places in your markup (such as inside JavaScript,) consult the OWASP XSS prevention cheat sheet.[10] There are a lot of surprising gotchas to allowing dynamic data throughout your markup.

Cross-Site Request Forgery (XSRF)

If XSS is a case of a browser trusting JavaScript from the server too much, XSRF is a case of a server trusting a browser too much.

---

9. http://blog.portswigger.net/2016/01/xss-without-html-client-side-template.html
10. https://www.owasp.org/index.php/XSS_(Cross_Site_Scripting)_Prevention_Cheat_Sheet

Let's go back to our example of a blogging site. Somehow there must be a browser request that saves a blog post to the server. Suppose the blog posting request looks something like this:

```
POST /blog/create HTTP/1.1
Host: www.romansjournalingsite.com
Accept-Encoding: gzip, deflate
Accept: */*
Cookie: sessionid=Re9ljf4uObKk9mSFqBlusxamUKw
Connection: keep-alive
Content-Type: application/x-www-form-urlencoded; charset=utf-8
Content-Length: 57

body=It+was+the+best+of+posts.+It+was+the+worst+of+posts.&submit=Publish
```

In a naive web application, that could be all it takes to publish to a hosted blog—a POST request with a logged-in sessionid cookie. Let's see how an attacker or an administrator of an evil website could use this for nefarious purposes.

Suppose I run a malicious website. I ostensibly serve up pictures of adorable kittens playing with yarn. But surreptitiously, I also serve up malicious content like this:

```
xsrf/kittens.html
<!DOCTYPE html>
<html lang="en">
<body>
  <form action="http://romansjournalingsite.com/post/create" method="POST">
    <input
      name=body
      value="Arbitrary Attacker-Controlled Content. I love evilxsrf.com"/>
    <input type=submit id=submit name=submit value=Publish />');
  </form>

  <script>
   document.getElementById('submit').click();
  </script>
</body>
```

What does this do? It creates a form with the action we just saw when we looked at the romansjournalingsite.com request that creates a new blog post. Additionally, the form is prepopulated with content that will create a blog post that says Arbitrary Attacker-Controlled Content. I love evilxsrf.com. Finally, it has JavaScript that automatically submits this form as soon as the page is loaded. This payload will cause a modern browser to make a POST request that looks like this:

```
POST /post/create HTTP/1.1
Host: romansjournalingsite.com
Content-Length: 74
Cache-Control: max-age=0
Origin: http://evilxsrf.com
Content-Type: application/x-www-form-urlencoded
Referer: http://evilxsrf.com/kittens.html
Accept-Encoding: gzip, deflate
Accept-Language: en-US,en;q=0.9
Cookie: sessionid=1234567890abcdef
Connection: close

body=Arbitrary+Attacker-Controlled+Content.+I+love+evilxsrf.com&submit=Publish
```

This looks just like the legitimate request! As far as romansjournalingsite.com is concerned, it *is* a legitimate request: it has a valid sessionid cookie. The admins of evilxsrf.com can use this to control the romansjournalingsite.com account of anyone who's logged in to romansjournalingsite.com and visits evilxsrf.com.

Just like we saw with XSS requests, this attack forges legitimate requests. They have a legitimate session ID, so the server will treat it as a legitimate request. The POST request wasn't generated because the user wanted to make that post, but the blog site can't tell that. The browser's same-origin policy (SOP) won't help here either. SOP only says that JavaScript from one site can't see responses sent back from other sites. But this attack doesn't require the JavaScript from the malicious site to see a response from the blogging site. This attack only requires that the JavaScript from the malicious site be able to POST a request to the blog site, which it can.

Romansjournalingsite.com needs to differentiate valid requests intentionally made by legitimite users from those that were made by malicious websites. Romansjournalingsite.com can't rely on session IDs or cookies, as we've seen. Romansjournalingsite.com needs to submit a little bit of secret data with every state-modifying request that only romansjournalingsite.com knows. This secret can't be stored in a cookie, though, because cookie values will be sent regardless of whether the request was initiated by a logged-in user or a malicious site operator. This leaves the form itself.

The defense against this is the XSRF hidden form input. When a user logs into the blog site, the blog site should set a large (say 128 bits, base64–encoded) cookie valid only for the duration of the session. Every page that contains a form that will POST back to the blog server needs to put that same value into a hidden form input. Only the blog site and the browser have this value. So when the user submits a valid POST to the blog site, this request will contain the anti-XSRF value, like this:

```
POST / HTTP/1.1
Host: localhost:1234
Accept-Encoding: gzip, deflate
Accept: */*
Connection: keep-alive
Cookie: antixsrf=XKRYopsd8jXj5DqgfNpHmA
Content-Type: application/x-www-form-urlencoded; charset=utf-8
Content-Length: 94

body=It+was+the+best+of+posts.+It+was+the+worst+of+posts.&submit=Publish&
antixsrf=XKRYopsd8jXj5DqgfNpHmA
```

So the form contains a hidden input whose value matches the xsrf cookie. If this form had been constructed by a malicious third-party website, the request would have looked like this:

```
POST / HTTP/1.1
Host: localhost:1234
Accept-Encoding: gzip, deflate
Accept: */*
Connection: keep-alive
Cookie: antixsrf=XKRYopsd8jXj5DqgfNpHmA
Content-Type: application/x-www-form-urlencoded; charset=utf-8
Content-Length: 72

body=It+was+the+best+of+posts.+It+was+the+worst+of+posts.&submit=Publish
```

That is, the POST request would have had the anti-XSRF cookie, because all requests to the blog site will contain the cookie. But the malicious website wouldn't be able to guess the value of the anti-XSRF cookie, and so it would not be able to replicate that value in the body of the request. If the server doesn't see the value in both places, the server can reject the request as a fake. At a minimum, requests like this should be denied and logged for later review.

Most modern web frameworks have defenses against XSRF. They may require additional development effort, however. So be sure to learn what your web development framework provides and use it on all state-modifying requests in your application. For example, there is good documentation on built-in XSRF defenses for ASP.NET,[11] Django,[12] and Ruby on Rails.[13]

---

11. https://docs.microsoft.com/en-us/aspnet/mvc/overview/security/xsrfcsrf-prevention-in-aspnet-mvc-and-web-pages
12. https://docs.djangoproject.com/en/2.0/ref/csrf/
13. http://guides.rubyonrails.org/security.html

There's an important caveat to XSRF defense. If the page is vulnerable to cross-site scripting (XSS), then the XSRF defenses will be bypassable. So it's important to make sure that our web applications are not vulnerable to XSS. To see why XSS can bypass XSRF defenses, let's think back to how XSRF defenses work. They add a little bit of secret information that wouldn't be exposed or sendable from other websites. Typically, this is done with a hidden form input. If there's XSS on a page with a hidden form input, malicious JavaScript can be injected into the page to send a request with the XSRF defense value.

XSRF Prevention with SameSite

We now have a very strong defense against XSRF—using an anti-XSRF hidden form input on all state-modifying requests. But that defense requires ongoing diligence. We're never done applying it. We need to reapply this defense every time we add a new state-modifying request to our web application (which will happen pretty often during active development of a web application). It would be nice if we could layer on a one-time effort to help lessen the impact if we ever forget to be diligent in the future. That is the idea behind SameSite cookies.[14] Let's take a look at this defense, how it helps, and what its limitations are.

Suppose we are building a web application that uses a cookie called SessionId to authenticate logged-in users. Normally, this cookie would be created by an HTTP response that includes a Set-Cookie header like this:

```
Set-Cookie: SessionId=sfVZ1yx68LD51I;
```

As we saw in the previous section on XSRF, if this cookie is the session cookie for our web application, it would then be sent on every request to our application, regardless of what site originated the request. Wouldn't it be nice if we could tell browsers to only send that cookie for requests that originated from our site? That's the idea behind SameSite.

With SameSite, the part of the response that sets the cookie would look like:

```
Set-Cookie: SessionId=sfVZ1yx68LD51I; SameSite=Strict;
```

or

```
Set-Cookie: SessionId=sfVZ1yx68LD51I; SameSite=Lax;
```

---

14. https://tools.ietf.org/html/draft-west-first-party-cookies-07

To understand this defense, we first need to understand a little bit of HTTP trivia. The HTTP specification defines "safe" and "unsafe" requests in Section 4.2.1 of RFC7231.[15] Safe requests use the GET, HEAD, OPTIONS, or TRACE methods. Unsafe requests use any of the other HTTP methods, including, most notably, POST requests. This distinction is there because the safe methods shouldn't change state on the server; only the unsafe ones should be used to modify state. It's the unsafe ones that we're concerned with when preventing XSRF.

Adding SameSite=Strict to a cookie definition tells a browser to never send that cookie for any request to our site unless the request originated from our site. That sounds good in practice, but it's often not what we want. With SameSite=Strict, other sites won't be able to link successfully to our web application because the initial request to our web application won't include the SessionId cookie since it originated from another site. If a user clicks on a link from another website to our web application, that first request would not include the SessionId cookie, so the user would probably be prompted to log in, even if they had already logged in. If you know that you don't need to support other sites linking to your web application, this would be an appropriate choice.

More often, what you want is to set SameSite=Lax. By doing this, all safe requests will send the cookie, even if the request originates from another site. This way, the initial link from an external site to our web application will send the SessionId cookie since clicking on the link will result in a GET request. But a malicious site that wants to exploit XSRF by constructing a form and getting a user to submit a POST request would fail because the SameSite attribute on the SessionId cookie wouldn't get sent because the request originated on another site.

So the addition of the SameSite attribute on our session cookie raises the bar for attackers in the event that we forget to implement XSRF defense in a new page in the future. Instead of being able to exploit the vulnerability by merely getting a logged-in user to browse to a website that the attacker controls, the attacker would need to find a DOM injection or XSS vulnerability in our web application in order to exploit the lack of XSRF defense.

Pretty cool. Now what are the limitations of this defense?

In describing the benefits of SameSite, we touched on the first limitation. SameSite doesn't protect you if your site is vulnerable to DOM injection or

---

15. https://tools.ietf.org/html/rfc7231#section-4.2.1

XSS. Put another way, if your site is dynamic enough to allow an attacker to submit HTML to be viewed by other users, then SameSite won't defend against XSRF attacks launched from within your own web application because all of the HTML and JavaScript is coming from the same site. It would still stop XSRF attacks initiated from other sites.

A second limitation is that the SameSite session cookie defense is dependent on support in the browser. Fortunately, it is widely supported.[16]

Finally, SameSite doesn't protect you if you allow safe methods to modify state. So if your website creates, updates, or deletes objects in your web application via safe methods, then SameSite will not protect you if you forget XSRF defenses.

Misconfiguration

> *Never attribute to malice that which is adequately explained by misconfiguration.*
> —Zabicki's Razor (with apologies to Hanlon)

Attackers are opportunistic. They won't bother with a sophisticated attack where a simple one will do, and seeking out and exploiting misconfigured systems is one of the simplest attacks there is.

We need to develop the capabilities for ongoing monitoring of our systems to make sure we haven't made the kinds of configuration mistakes that will open the door for easy attacks. The specifics of how you do this will vary significantly depending on exactly which technologies you use in your organization. We'll take a look at some of the most common misconfigurations and some tools to detect them. Even if you don't use these specific tools, these examples should give you an idea of the kinds of mistakes you'll want to be able to find.

Open S3 Buckets

Amazon[17] offers a popular storage service called Simple Storage Service, or S3 for short.[18] S3 is a large-scale key-value storage service that lets users store file-like "objects" inside of "buckets." A bucket can hold an arbitrary number of objects and an object can range in size up to 5TB. Behind the scenes, S3 is a highly durable storage service that automatically distributes data across multiple physical facilities. Amazon offers a lot of tools as well, including tools for big data analysis that integrate natively with S3.

---

16. https://caniuse.com/#search=samesite
17. https://aws.amazon.com
18. https://aws.amazon.com/s3/

It's really neat. It also seems to be really easy to misconfigure.

A quick Google search for "S3 breach" will show many high-profile instances of misconfigured S3 buckets that left sensitive data open for the world to see. No need for fancy attacks or cryptographic breakthroughs if the data isn't protected in the first place.

One particularly easy S3 mistake to make involves something called the Authenticated Users group. AWS permissions are based on group membership. So when setting up permissions, an administrator will typically create groups that represent the organization and assign permissions to those groups. The Authenticated Users group is a predefined group in AWS. It would be easy to look at the name and think that it describes the group of people that are authenticated users of one's own organization. That is not what that group means, however. Anyone who is logged into AWS as a part of any organization is automatically a member of the Authenticated Users group. If we look at the relevant documentation we read this:[19]

> When you grant access to the Authenticated Users group, any AWS-authenticated user in the world can access your resource.

And just below that, we see another predefined group called the All Users group. Amazon's documentation has this to say about the All Users group:

> Access permission to this group allows anyone in the world access to the resource. The requests can be signed (authenticated) or unsigned (anonymous).

So if you give the Authenticated Users group read access to your S3 buckets, you are giving read access to everyone in the world who has an AWS account. And any access you give to the All Users group is access you are also giving to everyone in the world, regardless of whether they have an AWS account or not.

The Authenticated Users and All Users group misconfigurations are a great example of the kind of misconfiguration we need to be able to detect. It's easy to see how they could be misused. It's easy to see the impact this could have. It's easy to see how their misuse could happen at any point in the life of an online system. It's easy to see how attackers could automate detection of this kind of misconfiguration and find this flaw in your system, even if they never had any reason to seek you out specifically.

A problem like this calls for automation. One tool that can help with finding misconfigurations like this is Scout2.[20] Scout2 is an open source tool designed

---

19. https://docs.aws.amazon.com/AmazonS3/latest/dev/acl-overview.html
20. https://github.com/nccgroup/Scout2

to look for a wide range of AWS misconfigurations, not just overly permissive S3 buckets. Installation and usage is outlined on the GitHub page and is fairly straightforward. Scout2 works by using AWS credentials that you provide to query the extensive AWS APIs to find common misconfigurations. It then takes the results of these queries and creates a report that summarizes its findings. At the time of this writing, it's still under active development with new misconfiguration searches being added periodically.

It only takes a couple of minutes to install and run Scout2. So if you use AWS, it's probably worthwhile to run it right now and see if you have anything pressing to fix before continuing on with this chapter.

I'll wait.

Now that you've run Scout2, it's worthwhile to budget some time to automate the regular generation of a Scout2 report. Even if everything is locked down perfectly today, mistakes could be introduced tomorrow. And if bad things happen in the future, it can be helpful to look back on a record of when things changed.

Default Passwords

Default passwords are another kind of misconfiguration that saves attackers a lot of time and effort. They're easy to exploit and easy to detect—just the kind of thing that attackers love. So we need to find them first. We can leverage the network inventory work we did in chapter 1 to give us a starting point for where to look. We'll also want to include network infrastructure like switches. We'll want to pay particular attention to anything that's exposed to the internet.

As was the case with defenses against SQL injection, our defense against this kind of misconfiguration can be layered. The first layer of the defense is to add to our provisioning checklist to make sure to not use default passwords when provisioning new services. Beyond that, we can look into scanning our network for default passwords. This second layer is highly specific to your network. You won't have time to exhaustively scan everything on your network. You'll need to use your judgment on where to focus your efforts. You may get a good return on looking into crusty old infrastructure that doesn't have clear ownership. And don't overlook networked printers. Networked printers can have capabilities like emailing or connecting to an Active Directory server. If you can get administrative access to a printer by using default credentials, you may be able to see the email or Active Directory credentials that enable those capabilities.

Care in avoiding default passwords can open the door for helpful monitoring as well. If possible, alert on failed login attempts that tried using default credentials. Once you've configured your system with new, nondefault credentials, there will never be a legitimate login attempt that uses the default credentials. If you see that someone has attempted a login with default credentials, you have a high-quality signal that an attack is under way.

Credentials

Checking credentials into a public GitHub repo is a common mistake. In the eyes of an attacker, leaked credentials are just as good as default credentials.

Even if we only use private source control servers, we still don't want to check credentials into source control. We don't want to have to do a build in order to change credentials. Also, putting credentials into source control makes it hard to introduce tiers of access. For instance, you may not want junior team members or third-party contractors to be able to see or change production credentials. Some organizational models call for a separation between those who write code and those who have access to run or deploy that code in production.

If we're agreed that keeping passwords out of source control is a good idea, it's worthwhile to have an automated way to enforce this in case we forget. If you have sensitive data confined to a single configuration file, you may be able to use features of your source control system to keep that file from ever getting checked in, even accidentally. Many source control systems can be configured to not track specific files. If you're using Git, you can add your sensitive configuration files to your .gitignore file.[21] This will keep you and your team from being able to check in the sensitive files at all. Other source control systems may offer similar functionality as well.

It's worthwhile to periodically look through our source code for credentials that have been checked in. This is especially important on a larger team. It's easy for decisions like not checking credentials into source control to not be communicated to the entire team, especially as the team grows over time.

The first tool you can use is just plain grep. It's worth doing a one-time manual search for words like the following:

- password
- cred
- token

```
grep -Ri password *
```

---

21. https://git-scm.com/docs/gitignore

These three words are worth scanning for, but you might get a lot of false positives. If you need to whittle down a lot of matches, you may want to filter these down. One way would be to look for occurrences that look like assignment statements in the programming language you use.

```
grep -Ri password * | grep '='
```

or

```
grep -Ri password * | grep ':' # if you use a lot of yaml or json
```

These next search patterns are very unlikely to have false positives. These are the beginnings of standard ssh private key files.

——BEGIN RSA PRIVATE KEY——

——BEGIN OPENSSH PRIVATE KEY——

——BEGIN DSA PRIVATE KEY——

——BEGIN EC PRIVATE KEY——

There are a number of tools that take this concept a little further. One example is TruffleHog.[22] One of the nice things about TruffleHog is that it understands Git. So point it at your Git repo and it will look for checked-in secrets on any check-in on any branch. The benefit is that it can find secrets even if they aren't in the latest branch. This catches the scenario where a developer accidentally checks in a password, realizes what they've done, then deletes the password on the next check-in. It's not enough to remove it from the latest branch, because as TruffleHog shows, an attacker with access to Git can go back through the check-in history and look for passwords that used to be checked in. TruffleHog has two modes of operation. One uses a configurable list of regex patterns, including the ssh private key patterns we looked at earlier. The second mode involves looking for high-entropy strings that "look" like checked-in certificates. The regex searches are faster and can be appropriate for adding into your build process.

Jenkins

If we use Jenkins,[23] we need to keep it patched, as we discussed back in Chapter 1, *Patching*, on page 1. But Jenkins has a common misconfiguration that merits special mention. Jenkins instances are often started with insecure settings that allow for unauthenticated execution of commands in a scripting

---

22. https://github.com/dxa4481/truffleHog
23. https://jenkins.io

language called Groovy.[24] Groovy scripts can execute arbitrary shell commands. So a common attack is to scan the network for misconfigured Jenkins servers, use the Groovy Scripting Console to dump passwords from the Jenkins server, then use those passwords to compromise other servers on the network. So make sure to lock down Jenkins so that it requires a login before allowing any of its functionality, especially the Groovy Scripting Console.

Public-Facing Servers

We're going to look at one last source of vulnerabilities in this chapter—long-forgotten public-facing servers. It's easy to forget to shut down public-facing servers that aren't used anymore. This mistake is even easier to make if you use a cloud-hosting service. We'll address the problem of forgotten or unpatched servers exposed to the internet similarly to the way we've addressed other vulnerabilities in this chapter. First, we'll do a one-time cleanup effort. Once we've addressed the problems of today, we'll add automation to make sure we don't reintroduce this problem again in the future.

Ideally, before you kick off a one-time cleanup effort, you already know exactly what servers you have exposed to the internet. Whether that's the case or not, it's worthwhile to examine your organization using a public tool. This can either serve as a first census or a double-check on your existing practices around maintaining an up-to-date inventory of your public-facing servers. The first time you do a check like this can be pretty eye-opening. You may be surprised to see how many public servers you actually maintain. You may also be surprised about how up-to-date the software running on those servers is. If these scans reveal version numbers of server-side software, be sure to google for CVEs for that software. We covered CVEs in *What Is a CVE?*, on page 3.

Two tools that are great for this are Shodan[25] and Censys.[26] Both Shodan and Censys continually scan the full IPv4 address space and provide queryable access to data about the servers they discover on the internet.

See what your organization has exposed to the internet. Hopefully there are no surprises there. Clean things up if there are. Then decide on a way to check automatically going forward. The amount of automation you will want to build out will be highly specific to your organization. If you only have a couple servers, maybe you can just manually look at your hosting service's

---

24. http://groovy-lang.org/
25. https://shodan.io
26. https://censys.io/

dashboard and eyeball it periodically. If you have a larger footprint or a larger organization with lots of people who can provision new servers, you'll probably want to put more effort into automating scans.

Suggested Reading

We've covered just some of the basics here. If you'd like to dig in deeper, I recommend reading the following:

- *The Art of Software Security Assessment [DMS06]* by Mark Dowd, John McDonald, and Justin Schuh
    - Read this for a more detailed look at a wide variety of coding mistakes that make software vulnerable to attack and their defenses.

- *The Web App Hacker's Handbook (2nd Edition) [SP11]* by Dafydd Stuttard and Marcus Pinto
    - This provides a more detailed look at web-specific attacks and their defenses.

- *The Hacker's Playbook (3rd Edition) [Kim18]* by Peter Kim
    - Kim gives you more ideas about where in your office network to look for vulnerabilities.

- "The Basics of Web Application Security" by Martin Fowler[27]
    - This article is a concise, general guide on how to write secure web-based software.

- Pushing Left, Like a Boss[28]
    - A great series of blog posts on how to adopt strong security practices earlier in the development cycle.

- DataSploit[29]
    - If you want to dig into what information is publicly available about the domains that your organization controls, take a look at DataSploit. This is an open source tool that queries a number of public repositories of information, including Shodan and Censys. It's designed to be used manually, but it also works nicely when called automatically. Scheduling it to run automatically on a regular basis and saving the output can give you a picture of how your public footprint has changed over time.

---

27. https://martinfowler.com/articles/web-security-basics.html
28. https://code.likeagirl.io/pushing-left-like-a-boss-part-1-80f1f007da95
29. https://github.com/DataSploit/datasploit

What's Next?

As we look back on the vulnerabilities we covered in this chapter, we see two main classes of vulnerabilities. In the first, an attacker is able to inject code of their own choosing into the system. In the second, operators accidentally leave the system in an insecure state. Interestingly, the defense for both looks fairly similar. First we make a one-time effort to find the vulnerabilities and fix them. We then layer on automated defenses to prevent mistakes from reintroducing the vulnerability. As teams and systems grow larger and older, we want to have more than vigilance keeping us from introducing vulnerabilities into the system; we want the system to prevent vulnerabilities from being introduced.

In our next chapter, we'll take a look at how we can use cryptography to secure the systems we build. We'll also see how seemingly small mistakes can let an attacker break weak cryptography. Just like a seemingly small flaw in our SQL allowed an attacker to bypass permission checks earlier in this chapter, seemingly small flaws in cryptography can leave our systems unprotected.

Here be dragons.

Anon.

CHAPTER 3

Cryptography

Cryptography is the sexiest topic in computer security. The word conjures up images of spies, adventures, and eccentric math geniuses. Move past the Hollywood take on cryptography, and you'll find that it really is a fascinating field. It ties together math, logic, low-level bit flipping, and even hardware design.

We aren't going to cover any of that.

Most coverage of cryptography starts with a discussion of prime numbers and the complexity of factoring composite numbers. This is done with an eye toward guiding you through implementing RSA encryption. This chapter will instead attempt to dissuade you from ever implementing any cryptography whatsoever. We'll see by example that implementing cryptography is too full of subtle mistakes for a newcomer to safely navigate.

To learn the subtleties and beauty of cryptography is a long, painstaking journey that is not the point of this chapter. Instead, let's stand on the shoulders of giants and use high-level crypto libraries with safe defaults.

The reader in a hurry can skip this chapter and just use NaCl,[1] libsodium,[2] or Tink[3] for encryption at rest. Use TLS 1.3 (or TLS 1.2 if you have legacy constraints) in a configuration that gets an *A* from SSL Labs[4] for data in transit. Use scrypt,[5] bcrypt,[6] PBKDF2,[7] or Argon2[8] for password hashing.

---

1.   https://nacl.cr.yp.to/
2.   https://libsodium.org/
3.   https://github.com/google/tink
4.   https://www.ssllabs.com/
5.   https://www.tarsnap.com/scrypt
6.   https://en.wikipedia.org/wiki/Bcrypt
7.   https://en.wikipedia.org/wiki/PBKDF2
8.   https://password-hashing.net/#argon2

In the rest of this chapter, we'll dive into the recommendations above. We'll also talk about safe password practices, including some precautions to take to soften the blow in case an attacker should ever get access to our credentials.

Don't Roll Your Own Crypto

Writing cryptography software isn't like writing regular software. When writing regular software, little bugs tend to have little impacts. If you have an off-by-one bug, you could expect a small bug, for example, omitting one result on a search page. If you forget to check for null references, maybe a program crashes. But with cryptography, a small mistake may leave you with a system that encrypts and decrypts correctly for well-intentioned inputs but fails entirely when faced with malicious input. The developer needs to either redis-cover the entire field from scratch or subject the code to the scrutiny of others with a deep understanding of the field. Just as you can't tickle yourself, you can't find the mistakes you've made that involve flaws you haven't learned about yet. Bruce Schneier has a nice essay on Schneier's Law that expands on this.[9]

There are many different attack models to consider. A common, though mis-guided, mental model of a secure crypto system is one where the attacker gets to see a single message of modest length. If the attacker can decrypt it, then the system is insecure; otherwise it's suitable for any and all purposes. That certainly is an attack that a crypto system should be able to defend against. But there are many other models to consider, such as the following:

- An attacker who can listen to many encrypted messages between two parties

- An attacker who can replay previously transmitted encrypted messages

- An attacker who can replay modified variants of previously transmitted encrypted messages

- An attacker who can replay modified variants of previously transmitted encrypted messages to a recipient who's expecting only well-behaved communication and who therefore displays helpful error messages if anything goes wrong during decryption

- An attacker who can listen to the encrypted communication between two parties where some of the plaintexts are known to the attacker

- An attacker who can influence the contents of encrypted communication between two other parties

---

9.   https://www.schneier.com/blog/archives/2011/04/schneiers_law.html

Defenses that protect against more limited adversaries may fail against more advanced adversaries.

It's easy to see all of the security breaches in the news and decide to protect ourselves by building a new kind of encryption. That's a laudable goal, but it's misguided. Without a deep understanding of how systems have been compromised, it's unlikely that someone would be able to design a safer system from first principles. Better to reign in that desire to build a new crypto system until you have broken a couple yourself. If you haven't broken anything yet, you are likely to just repeat other people's mistakes from the past. As the saying goes,

> Those who do not learn history are destined to have George Santayana quoted at them.

Fields, Kerckhoffs, and Shannon

It always catches my attention when I see similar advice from multiple traditions. It feels like triangulating in on the truth.

Linguist and cryptographer Auguste Kerckhoffs is best known for a pair of essays written in 1883. The key piece of advice from these essays is known these days as Kerckhoffs's Law, one translation of which is, "A cryptosystem should be secure even if everything about the system, except the key, is public knowledge."

Electrical engineer and cryptographer Claude Elwood Shannon made fundamental advances to circuit design and information encoding. He played an important role in American cryptography during World War II and worked with Alan Turing. Of particular interest to us is Shannon's Maxim, "The enemy knows the system."

It's not really a surprise that two early pioneers in cryptology would have such similar advice for us. What catches my eye, however, is how well this fits in with a lesson from W.C. Fields, a famous comedian, entertainer, and perhaps security researcher. Fields coined a famous saying that I like to call Fields's Imperative: "Never give a sucker an even break." (NGASAEB)

Fields's Imperative reminds us that when we're building a system, our design determines what the adversary has to achieve in order to defeat it. If we build a system that relies on the secrecy of the implementation for its security, we're giving the adversary an even break. Kerckhoffs and Shannon told us that we should expect our adversaries to understand our implementation.

Consider how hard you'd have to work to make sure an adversary could never do any of the following:

- Find your backups

- Find your source control

- Find a disgruntled current or former developer

- Threaten or bribe a gruntled current or former developer

- Compromise a single computer that runs your software and then decompile the software

- Watch network traffic

Why bring this up? Because people who roll their own crypto commonly arrive at designs that assume a secret implementation and don't provide security if the adversary understands the implementation.

For further evidence of Kerckhoffs's Law and Shannon's Maxim, look at NaCl and Tink. They show that it's possible to be secure while also disclosing the full implementation.

Another way of looking at this is to ask yourself what the adversary would need to do in order to win. Are you content to let the adversary win if all they need to do is decompile your program? Or if all they need to do is see your source code? No! Don't set the bar that low. Never give a sucker an even break!

So what is modern cryptography built on? How does it provide security even while letting the implementation be known to the adversary?

Modern cryptography is built out of mathematical problems that appear to have no efficient solutions. To take one example, the security of RSA encryption is based on the difficulty of factoring large numbers. That is, given a large number x, find two numbers y and z such that $x = y * z$. In grammar school we learn how to take y and z and multiply them together to get x. But going the other way and splitting x into $y * z$ appears to be difficult. We can do it, but not always efficiently. It's easy to factor 35, for instance. By the time you finish reading this sentence, you'll probably have figured out that 35 can be represented as $5 * 7$. You probably did this by either remembering your multiplication tables or trying to divide 35 by each integer up through 5. Try that approach on a number with hundreds of digits (as is the case in RSA), and you'll see quickly that this approach works slowly. Mathematicians have been working on this problem for centuries but haven't come up with anything terribly efficient. Mathematicians' tears are the best basis for cryptographic systems.

What does the adversary need to do to win? If your answer isn't as good as "Make a fundamental advance to mathematics that has eluded mathematicians for centuries," then you're better off not rolling your own crypto.

Security When the Enemy Knows the System

So if the entire implementation of our crypto systems is known to the adversary, how can we be secure? The adversary can just run our code after all.

The key is key. Encryption algorithms don't just take plain text as input, they take a key as well. A well-written encryption algorithm will produce wildly different outputs when encrypting a given plaintext with keys that differ only slightly. The key is the only part that needs to be kept secret. Rather than keeping an entire algorithm secret, we just need to keep our key secret.

An encryption algorithm should be so strong that even if an attacker had full access to the source code, the attacker would have no better option than to brute force all possible passwords. We won't cover how the encryption libraries recommended in this chapter achieve this goal. We'll merely note that they've been found to do so. If we've built a system like this, all the implementer has to do is to pick a suitably large random encryption key. Encryption keys are commonly 256 bits. That means that there are 2^256 possible values for an encryption key. That's 2 * 2 * ... * 2, or 256 2s all multiplied together. 2^256 is an awfully big number. How big? Well, it's even bigger than the number of different ways you can order a standard deck of playing cards. There are about 8.06 x 10^67 (or 8 followed by 67 zeroes) different ways to order a deck of playing cards. The number 2^256 is about 1.15 x 10^77 (or 1 followed by 77 zeroes). So there are about 1.4 billion times more 256-bit encryption keys than there are ways to order a standard deck of playing cards.

\//   **Joe asks:**
ᒨ   # What's So Great About a Deck of Playing Cards?

I have to turn your attention to one of the most fun bits of math I've ever read.[a] It's a great way to help visualize just how many different ways you can order a standard deck of playing cards. When you order a deck, there are 52 possibilities for the first card. You pick the first one, and that leaves 51 possibilities for the second card, 50 for the third card, and so on. That makes for 52 * 51 * 50 * ... * 4 * 3 * 2 * 1 different possibilities. The shorthand for this is 52! (pronounced "52 factorial") and it's so big, that, well, just read the linked story. It's fun.

---

a.   czep.net/weblog/52cards.html

Kerckhoffs's and Shannon's advice comes primarily from witnessing firsthand the futility of keeping implementations secret. An additional benefit to building systems where the only secret is the key is that it's really hard to keep secrets. If a password is compromised, suspected of being compromised, or has just been in use for too long, a secure system should be able to replace it with a new one and recover. (The problem of discovering what, if anything, an adversary did with compromised passwords and recovering from that is outside the scope of this book.)

Consider the relative difficulty of changing out all the passwords in a system versus the difficulty of changing out the entire system itself.

Don't Use Low-Level Crypto Libraries

Hopefully we're now in agreement that we shouldn't roll our own crypto. It might seem that all we need to do is grab a low-level encryption library and start using its AES encryption and decryption functions. After all, that's not "rolling our own crypto."

As we'll see in this next section, low-level encryption libraries present a lot of configuration choices that are easy to misuse. For example, many low-level cryptography libraries provide support for outdated algorithms like MD5 and 3DES. And oftentimes comparisons of libraries such as Wikipedia's show supported algorithms in a way makes it seem as though libraries with support for more algorithms are fuller featured.[10] Low-level libraries don't provide guidance; instead they force the developer to know which algorithms are safe to use. Even if the developer knows to choose a strong encryption algorithm like AES, low-level cryptography libraries still provide dangerous configuration choices. These choices include things like block mode and key size. Getting these choices wrong can result in a system that's insecure. In contrast, a high-level encryption library is opinionated and makes these configuration choices for the developer. This makes a high-level encryption library misuse-resistant.

Let's take a look at some of the ways it's possible to misuse low-level encryption libraries.

AES and the ECB Penguin

AES.

Have there ever been three letters that give such a feeling of safety? AES, or the Advanced Encryption Standard, has a strong pedigree. Initially called

---

10. https://en.wikipedia.org/wiki/Comparison_of_cryptography_libraries

Rijndael, after its creators, Vincent Rijmen and Joan Daemen, it earned the name AES after being named the finalist in the National Institute of Standards and Technology (NIST) selection process. This selection process took several years and pitted fifteen competing algorithms against each other. During that process and after its selection, the AES algorithm has withstood tremendous scrutiny from a tremendous number of talented cryptographers. It is the only publicly known algorithm recommended by the United States' National Security Agency (NSA) for government secrets classified TOP SECRET.[11] It seems no advertising copy for secure software is complete without a mention of the "bank-grade" or "military-grade" encryption it provides. And use of AES brings a sense of relief from having satisfied those smug crypto nerds by not writing new crypto.

But it's really easy to misuse.

AES is a block cipher. Probably the easiest way to misuse AES is to pick the wrong block mode.

So what's a block mode and what's a block cipher?

A block cipher takes two inputs—a plaintext to be encrypted and a key with which to encrypt the plaintext. It uses the key to encrypt the plaintext and produce a ciphertext. The input plaintext, the key, and the output are by definition all the same length. If you only ever had 256 bits of data to encrypt, you couldn't ask for a better way than by using AES. As it is, however, we generally have more than 256 bits of data to encrypt.

A block mode is a set of rules that defines how to use an encryption algorithm that works on a single block in order to encrypt plaintext of arbitrary length. Choice of block mode is orthogonal to the choice of encryption algorithm, so you can use the AES algorithm with any block mode. We'll take a look at two block modes—electronic code book (ECB) and cipher block chaining (CBC).

We'll start with ECB because it's the simplest block mode and is the default block mode in many libraries. In ECB mode, the first block of plaintext is encrypted by itself. Then the next block of plaintext is encrypted by itself, and so on. A padding operation is used to add on data so that the final block is also a full block. The ciphertext is just the concatenation of encrypting each block of the plaintext individually. It's the straightforward approach you'd first think of when thinking about how to apply an operation that works on a fixed-size block to a plaintext of arbitrary length.

---

11. https://csrc.nist.gov/projects/cryptographic-standards-and-guidelines/archived-crypto-projects/aes-development

Suppose you were encrypting HTML and you had this plaintext:

```
<td class="foo">
```

which is 16 bytes, or 128 bits long. When encrypted under a 128-bit key, K, suppose this encrypts to the following in hex:

```
0000000 4c 69 63 65 6e 73 65 2e 74 78 74 0a 52 45 41 44
```

So far, so good. The only problem is that if we ever encounter plaintext block

```
<td class="foo">
```

again in this same message, that block will be encrypted into the same ciphertext that was generated last time we saw this plaintext.

```
0000000 4c 69 63 65 6e 73 65 2e 74 78 74 0a 52 45 41 44
```

This follows from encrypting each block as a completely isolated operation. Every time a given plaintext block is encrypted within a single message, it will encrypt to the same ciphertext because there are only two inputs to the encryption operation—the key and the plaintext block. Since the key is the same for the entire message, it's clear that repeated blocks of plaintext will encrypt to the same ciphertext. This leads to repeating patterns in the ciphertext.

To see how this could create problems, consider a picture of Tux, the lovable Linux penguin, created in 1996 by Larry Ewing using the GIMP.[12] It contains many blocks that contain just white pixels, which encrypt to one ciphertext, and many blocks that contain just black pixels, which encrypt to another ciphertext.

---

12. https://commons.wikimedia.org/wiki/File:Tux.png

When we encrypt Tux in AES-ECB mode,[13] the resulting ciphertext is only somewhat obfuscated, even though it has been encrypted with military-grade AES encryption.

Sometimes people respond to this kind of flaw by asking questions like "But what about other file types? What if I zip the plaintext first?" or "What if my plaintext doesn't have this much redundancy?" Don't be tempted into thinking that maybe ECB is okay this one time. Don't go down the rabbit hole of contorting your applications to try to work with weak cryptography. Just use strong cryptography. Remember Fields's Imperative—never give a sucker an even break! Also think of the junior dev who will follow in your footsteps. Even if you really do have a grasp of cryptography that allows you to find a use case where ECB isn't a terrible mistake, your successors likely will not. "That's how we did it before" has enormous influence on later development. Don't tempt future maintainers of your code to use ECB.

ECB Malleability

Malleability is another problem with ECB mode. A crypto system that's malleable is one that allows for an attacker to take parts of one or more encrypted messages and combine them to forge a new message.

Remember that each block of the plaintext is encrypted completely independently, and each block of ciphertext is decrypted completely independently. So let's say we have an application that maintains a list of admin accounts,

---

13. https://commons.wikimedia.org/wiki/File:Tux_ecb.jpg

followed by the delimiter "Banned user list," followed by a list of banned users. And for security purposes, let's suppose that it was decided to encrypt this list on disk using AES-ECB. If the legitimate plaintext was this:

```
admin1@bigco.com
admin2@bigco.com
intern@bigco.com
Banned user list
notnice@abcd.com
mean@website.com
```

Suppose this encrypts to this:

```
00000000: 6e42 96b1 47ae 6963 0e26 7cc8 883e 1074  nB..G.ic.&|..>.t
00000010: 57ee 68e0 48d4 f5d7 a463 9fd7 394a 5a72  W.h.H....c..9JZr
00000020: 2d01 60eb 9e76 919e 46e1 eede b015 f657  -.`..v..F......W
00000030: 7610 6ab4 8c4d 2fad 3390 c051 4fa7 0964  v.j..M/.3..QO..d
00000040: e9c1 300c da3d 9d8f df70 4779 c8f0 e413  ..0..=...pGy....
00000050: d2a8 ac73 14b4 1d8a 86a7 0f77 c38a b4db  ...s.......w....
```

An attacker can just rearrange the blocks so that the last two blocks are first, followed by the delimiter, and then finally the legitimate admins. It will decrypt this just fine. This will put the banned users in the admin list and ban all the legitimate admins! From this example we can see that, depending on the structure of the plaintext, many kinds of edits are possible—including repeating, deleting, and reordering blocks—without knowing the key.

This may seem contrived. What about block boundaries? The attack in this example works because the delimiter and the email addresses were aligned on block boundaries. Yes, the specific email addresses were contrived to work in a quick example. But the principle still holds. In the general case, it may take a bit more effort to rearrange the blocks so that it decrypts correctly. The attacker is aided by the fact that many file formats allow for a fair amount of malleability in the form of things like comments, whitespace, and no-ops, so it's often possible. But nothing in AES-ECB prevents it.

Let's consider a second scenario. Consider a naive web application with a complex permissions model. For performance reasons, the developers have decided not to query the database for permissions on every request to this web application. Instead, at login time, and every time permissions change for a given user, the application issues a cookie whose value is an encrypted list of all the permissions that the user is granted. If this value were encrypted with ECB, a malicious user could learn about the structure of the web application and slice together pieces of several cookies they may have been issued over time and construct a new cookie for themselves that grants them administrative privileges. The previous section listed several ways an attacker could learn more about the structure of the cookie's value. Even without access to the source code, an attacker could start to learn about the structure of the cookie without any access to source. An attacker could create multiple users and compare their cookies. An attacker could possibly change metadata about their account through the application and observe the change in the cookie.

CBC Is Still Malleable

It may seem like the moral of this story is that ECB mode is terrible and that if you just avoid ECB mode you're all set. So what mode would you pick then? CBC mode is widely used and is a default choice in some widely used crypto libraries. That might be a good choice, right? Well, CBC mode has flaws and should be avoided in new development.

CBC gets around ECB's problem with repeated plaintext blocks by using an initialization vector, or IV. An IV is another input to an encryption operation that's the same length as the block size. So instead of having this:

```
encrypt(plaintext, key)
```

We have this:

```
encrypt(plaintext, iv, key)
```

By using a unique initialization vector each time a message is encrypted with a given key, repeated blocks in the plaintext will be encrypted to different blocks in the ciphertext.

This can be seen more easily with a picture. In the following figure,[14] we see that the IV is XOR'd with the first block of the plaintext.

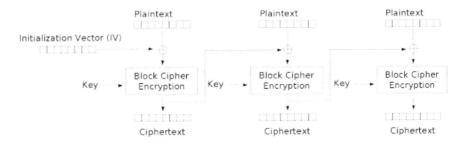

Cipher Block Chaining (CBC) mode encryption

---

14. https://en.wikipedia.org/wiki/Block_cipher_mode_of_operation#Cipher_Block_Chaining_(CBC)

The result of XORing the first block of the plaintext with the IV is then encrypted with AES. So even if all three plaintext blocks were identical, they'll each be XOR'd with something different before being encrypted, so the ciphertext will not retain a pattern like we saw with Tux in the ECB example. More specifically, the first plaintext block will be XOR'd with the IV before encryption. The second plaintext block will be XOR'd with the first ciphertext block. The third plaintext block will be XOR'd with the second ciphertext block.

This improvement over ECB mode sounds pretty good. CBC ciphertexts don't retain patterns from the plaintext. This improvement is necessary but not sufficient for safe use.

CBC mode is probably good enough for the mental model that most readily jumps into people's minds when thinking up new crypto schemes. If you, as an attacker, were faced with a single ciphertext generated by AES-CBC-256 encryption, you probably couldn't eyeball it and produce its plaintext. But that isn't the bar we need to clear.

CBC mode encryption fails in the face of an active attacker who can see encrypted traffic and use that to forge new messages.

Suppose I am an active attacker and I have a three-block CBC cipher text and I want to alter the third block of the resulting plaintext. I could alter bytes of the third block of ciphertext, but that doesn't help me because I don't know how those alterations will change the third block of plaintext. But what if I can "sacrifice" the second block? Suppose I don't care what the second block of the plaintext is. In this case, since I can submit any arbitrary ciphertext I want, I can use the second block as an IV for the third block. So if I want to flip the fifth bit of the third block, I can do that by flipping the fifth bit of the second block of the ciphertext.

This allows an attacker to "sacrifice" the *n_th block of plaintext in exchange for having complete control over the (_n*+1)th block of plaintext. For a more dramatic explanation of this attack, read the excellent short story ["If You're Typing the Letters A-E-S Into Your Code You're Doing It Wrong" by Thomas Ptacek.[15]

This is another application of Fields's Imperative, "Never give a sucker an even break." A first reaction to problems with ECB or CBC might be to play with the plaintext to obscure patterns in it before encrypting, or to try and

15. https://www.nccgroup.trust/us/about-us/newsroom-and-events/blog/2009/july/if-youre-typing-the-letters-a-e-s-into-your-code-youre-doing-it-wrong/

find a reason that the attacks aren't applicable. Resist that impulse. Instead of working around flawed cryptography, get rid of flawed cryptography altogether. Even if you account for all the publicly known attacks today, you're building on shaky ground. Cryptography attacks never get worse over time, they only become more efficient. What today seems like leaking a couple bits of information may turn into a complete system failure with tomorrow's research. And even if you have sufficient mitigating controls this one time, you're setting a dangerous example for the future.

It turns out that a lot of the commonly used block modes are broken. All of the nonauthenticated ones have these kinds of problems. And even if you move into authenticated modes, there are still lots of pitfalls. There's correct choice of nonces, side channel attacks, and lots of other attacks besides. It's just too easy to make mistakes. If you don't have the experience in the field, you won't know to test for these kinds of vulnerabilities, either.

The fine folks behind Cryptopals have summed this up beautifully.[16]

> The current state of crypto software security is similar to the state of software security in the 1990s. Specifically: until around 1995, it was not common knowledge that software built by humans might have trouble counting. As a result, nobody could size a buffer properly, and humanity incurred billions of dollars in cleanup after a decade and a half of emergency fixes for memory corruption vulnerabilities.

> Counting is not a hard problem. But cryptography is. There are just a few things you can screw up to get the size of a buffer wrong. There are tens, probably hundreds, of obscure little things you can do to take a cryptosystem that should be secure even against an adversary with more CPU cores than there are atoms in the solar system, and make it solvable with a Perl script and 15 seconds. Don't take our word for it: do the challenges and you'll see.

In conclusion, use NaCl,[17] libsodium,[18] or Tink.[19]

If you're interested in learning more about terrifyingly easy mistakes to make in implementing cryptography, I can't recommend Cryptopals highly enough. It contains a fascinating and illuminating series of cryptography puzzles that show how seemingly reasonable implementation choices can have disastrous consequences. It will put you off crypto development for good. And, as a extra bonus, it can be a great way to learn a new (or even a first) programming language.

---

16. https://cryptopals.com
17. https://nacl.cr.yp.to/
18. https://libsodium.org/
19. https://github.com/google/tink

Evaluating Crypto Libraries Without Being a Crypto Expert

So now we've ruled out low-level crypto libraries. What should we use instead? High-level crypto libraries with secure defaults written by experts.

But how do we know experts when we see them? Evaluating people based on skills we don't have ourselves is a tough problem with no great solution. We encounter it in other parts of our life. How do we evaluate doctors, mechanics, lawyers, plumbers, and other specialists with skills we don't have? We tend to use a few techniques. We can look for professionals with certifications. Sometimes we can look for professionals who have written helpful books, articles, or blog posts. We ask our friends or look to the wisdom of crowds and check ratings online. When we apply any of these, we find folks like Bernstein and Lange (authors of NaCl) and Bleichenbacher and Duong (authors of Tink) pass with flying colors. But since we're in cryptography, we have one more technique we can bring to bear. When we evaluate a library, we can look at the track record of its authors. What have they broken? What have they built and how has that held up to scrutiny? Add this metric, and you'll find Bernstein, Lange, Bleichenbacher, and Duong have about as impressive a trophy case as you're going to find.

So what have the authors of these libraries done that should inspire confidence?

Bernstein and Lange are accomplished academics with a strong body of work. In addition, their work on NaCl has stood up to widespread scrutiny for many years. NaCl uses Bernstein's Salsa20 cipher extensively.[20] Bernstein's related ChaCha20 cipher[21] has been used by Google[22] for securing TLS communication since 2014, which is a nice compliment on the strength of ChaCha20. Additionally, Bernstein's earlier work on programs such as djbdns and qmail has also stood up to widespread usage and scrutiny for many years.

Daniel Bleichenbacher is most famous for the "Bleichenbacher attack" against RSA.[23] He first described this attack in 1998. His attack allows for decrypting RSA encryption without direct access to the decryption key. Twenty years later, this attack is still relevant. It was the inspiration for Hanno Böck, Juraj Somorovsky, and Craig Young's ROBOT (Return Of Bleichenbacher's Oracle

---

20. https://cr.yp.to/snuffle.html
21. https://cr.yp.to/chacha.html
22. https://security.googleblog.com/2014/04/speeding-up-and-strengthening-https.html
23. https://web.archive.org/web/20120204040056/http://www.bell-labs.com/user/bleichen/papers/pkcs.ps

Threat) attack.[24] The ROBOT attack even won the 2018 Pwnie award for Best Cryptographic Attack.[25]

Thai Duong codiscovered the BEAST,[26] CRIME,[27] and POODLE[28] vulnerabilities in SSL/TLS. The BEAST attack, discovered by Duong and Rizzo, allows an an eavesdropper to decrypt TLS 1.0 communication. Its discovery was a major factor in the adoption of the TLS 1.1 standard. The CRIME attack, also discovered by Duong and Rizzo, leverages HTTP compression to decrypt HTTPS traffic to steal cookies and hijack sessions. Finally, we have the POODLE attack, discovered by Bodo Möller, Thai Duong, and Krzysztof Kotowicz. POODLE allows a man-in-the-middle attack during the TLS handshake that allows the attacker to downgrade what would have been a TLS connection between a browser and a server to a much weaker SSL 3.0 connection.

So when we look at the achievements of these four library authors, we can have more confidence in their implementations and configuration choices than we'd have in some other library chosen at random. They're only human and can certainly make mistakes just like anyone else. But we can be pretty sure that, at the very least, their libraries won't be vulnerable to the attacks that the authors are famous for.

We haven't talked about the authors of libsodium. They're smart people as well, but we don't need to focus on their careers as much because they're porting NaCl, not designing a system from scratch. So we don't have to trust their API choices, just their implementation abilities.

NaCl, libsodium, and Tink are high-level cryptography libraries. When we look at their APIs, we see that the authors have made all of the low-level design choices for us. We don't have an opportunity to choose or misconfigure obscure cryptographic settings. This combination of a misuse-resistant API and distinguished authors is what makes these libraries good choices.

This takes care of how we encrypt and decrypt arbitrary data. As we'll see in the next section, encryption and decryption aren't what we want for storing the passwords of our clients. Instead of encryption, which is reversible if we have the password, we'll want to use one-way algorithms that can't be reversed aside from brute forcing.

---

24. https://robotattack.org/

25. https://pwnies.com/

26. https://en.wikipedia.org/wiki/Transport_Layer_Security#BEAST_attack

27. https://docs.google.com/presentation/d/11eBmGiHbYcHR9gL5nDyZChu_-lCa2GizeuOfaLU2HOU/
    edit#slide=id.g1de53288_0_16

28. https://www.openssl.org/~bodo/ssl-poodle.pdf

Password Storage

Our users' passwords are extremely valuable to attackers. An attacker with access to user passwords pretty much has full control of our application. Such an attacker will probably be able to gain access to many other systems as well: unfortunately, people frequently use the same passwords on multiple websites. We'll obviously do everything we can to prevent compromise. But if we fail in that, we can take an important precaution to lower the value of our users' passwords—we won't store the user passwords at all. Instead, we'll use a cryptographic hashing algorithm so that we store a value that's derived from the password.

We're going to start with a brief discussion of hashing and then walk through a brief history of password-storage techniques.

On Storing (and Not Storing) Your Users' Passwords

Instead of storing a user password, we can store a value that's derived from the password itself. If this derivation can only be performed in one direction (that is, it's easy to calculate the derived value given a password but it's hard to go from a derived value back to the original password), then we'll have a great defense. When a user creates an account for themselves, they'll enter a password and we won't store the password itself, we'll only store the derived value. Next time the user logs in, they'll type in their password, we'll perform that same derivation and compare it to the previously stored derived value. If the two derived values match, we know the user typed in the right password. If they don't match, we know the user typed in the wrong password. At no time do we ever store the user password itself, only the derived value. This helps us in the unfortunate event that an attacker gets access to our database. Knowing the derived value of a password doesn't help an attacker log in, because if they type in the derived value when they attempt to log in, the system will derive a value from the derived value, and that won't match the derived value of the real password, so the attacker won't be able to log in. These derived values are much less valuable to an attacker.

This talk of derived values is a little magical and hand-wavy, so let's talk about real-life derivations. A hashing function has the properties that we're looking for. Hashing functions have been thoroughly researched in academia and widely used in industry. Hashing algorithms have a long history of use in preventing and detecting accidental corruption of data from unreliable networks and file systems. More recently, they've been cleverly applied to the problem of password storage. A hashing algorithm takes an arbitrary-length input and maps it into a fixed-length bucket called a hash code. The mapping of arbitrary-length input to hash code is said to be "one-way" only. That is, it's easy to calculate a hash code for any input. But it's "hard" to calculate the reverse of this and find an input given only a hash code. In this case, by "hard" we're using the academic modesty of computer science—there are no known ways to reverse any of the widely used hash algorithms other than to try all of the possible inputs and see which one matches the given hash code.

So if we pick a hashing algorithm that produces hash codes that are uniformly distributed over a very large number of possible outputs, we have the beginning of a secure way to store our user passwords.

Let's take a look at a concrete example—the popular SHA-256 hashing algorithm. SHA-256 takes input of any size and maps it into an output of 256 bits (32 bytes). It's kind of crazy that you could take a really large input, like all the data on a 50-GB Blu-ray disc, and map it into just 32 bytes. The thing to remember is that this operation is not compression because it is not reversible. Given a 256-bit hash, you can't tell if the input that generated it is small or large or whether it was a Blu-ray, text, gif, or something else, and you can't work backward to find the input that generated it.

Recall that back in *What's So Great About a Deck of Playing Cards?*, on page 59, we saw that the number of different 256-bit strings is really big. Large numbers are necessary, but not sufficient, to keep passwords safe. To see why that is, let's take a look at how attacks and defenses have leapfrogged each other over the years.

Store Passwords in the Clear

Initially, passwords were just stored in the clear on the server. The thinking was that an attacker who got as far as being able to read from the database had already "won," so why bother doing anything else? You can see evidence of this having been a trend if you think back to websites in the 1990s and early 2000s. It was common practice at the time for websites to email passwords back to users who clicked on the "I forgot my password" button.

With passwords stored in the clear in a database, an attacker who gets database access, say, through SQL injection, can exfiltrate the passwords of every user of the system. This is a big problem, especially since people tend to reuse passwords across websites. So a breach at one site could impact many other sites that have no vulnerabilities at all.

Reversibly Encrypt Everyone's Passwords

One weak response to this threat is to encrypt all passwords before storing them in the database. But it's weak because the master password that allows the system to decrypt all of the user passwords has to be known to the system. If it weren't, the system would not be able to log anyone in. So this defense only helps in a very narrow set of circumstances.

Store Hash of Passwords

The important insight for secure password storage is to realize that you never have to store the password itself. Instead, you can store a value that's derived from the password. You need a derivation that's extremely unlikely to generate the same derived value for two different inputs.

Initially, people used this insight by storing the output of generic hashing algorithms like MD5 and SHA-1 instead of the password itself. Then, when a user logged in, the hash output of the user-supplied input was compared to the previously stored hash output from when the user was created. If they're the same, then the user is logged in. This was a step forward because the passwords themselves no longer had to be stored. So if the database were compromised, the passwords weren't given up to the attacker directly.

Rainbow Tables

For a time, the best an attacker could hope to do with password hashes was to look them up via rainbow tables. Rainbow tables are generated by hashing each ASCII input up to a certain length and storing the input and the hash so that one can look up an ASCII input given a hash. Rainbow tables take up a lot of space, and they take a lot of time to build. For example, there are 95 printable ASCII characters. If you want to generate the hashes for all printable passwords up to 8 characters in length, there are

$$(95)+(95^2)+(95^3)+(95^4)+(95^5)+(95^6)+(95^7)+(95^8) == 6,704,780,954,517,120$$
$$\sim= 6.7 \times 10^{15}$$

different printable 8-character passwords. That's over 6 quadrillion. (I had to look up what comes after trillion.) Storing all of these takes up quite a lot of space. A SHA-256 hash is 64 bytes, so storing just the hashes takes up approximately 429,105,981,089,095,700 bytes, or approximately 399,636,087 GB or approximately 381 PB.

Now if your password is chosen from a smaller alphabet, say just the lowercase English alphabet, the storage requirements drop dramatically to

(26)+(26^2)+(26^3)+(26^4)+(26^5)+(26^6)+(26^7)+(26^8) == 217,180,147,158 ~= 2.17 x 10^11

or approximately 202 GB. Hence a lot of the advice from this period was to choose a password with at least one uppercase, one lowercase, one numeric, and one non-alphanumeric character.

So rainbow tables are cumbersome and were even more cumbersome in decades gone by. But even with modern computers, we can see that the exponential growth of adding additional characters to passwords would make rainbow tables impractical. Even if we use the lowly lowercase English alphabet for our password, by extending the password length out to 15 characters, we get a staggering

(26^15) == 1,677,259,342,285,725,925,376 ~= 1.6 x 10^21

That's 5 orders of magnitude bigger than the key space of all printable ASCII passwords up to 8 characters in length. So the storage requirements for a rainbow table for 15-character passwords of just lowercase letters would be about 5 orders of magnitude larger, or about 95,341,155 PB. Wouldn't it be cool if we could make all the passwords longer? That would make us pretty safe against rainbow tables. This is the insight behind salts.

A salt is a nonsecret value that is stored in the clear adjacent to the password. We should assume that an adversary who can read hashed passwords can also read the salt. The salt is concatenated with the plaintext password before hashing. This renders the rainbow table ineffective. If you just pick a salt of, say 14 characters, you know that even if a user managed to choose a one-character password (you should prevent this, by the way!), the adversary would need a rainbow table that contained at least 26^15, or 1.6 x 10^21 different passwords in order to attack this password, and we just saw that this requires about 95,341,155 PB of storage, so we can see that salting makes rainbow tables completely impractical.

But no one should care about merely stopping rainbow table attacks because there are much more efficient attack vectors nowadays.

GPUs

Moore's Law has altered the landscape in this cat-and-mouse game.[29] The problem with using general-purpose hashing algorithms for password hashing

---

29. https://en.wikipedia.org/wiki/Moore%27s_law

is that general-purpose hashing algorithms are designed to be really fast. And Moore's Law makes them faster all the time. Salting doesn't increase the number of possibilities that need to be checked; salting only changes the set of possibilities that need to be checked from one population (all the printable passwords under, say, 10 characters) to another (that same set of passwords, each prefixed with the same prefix or salt.) This is very parallelizable and a great task for the many cores in a graphical processing unit (GPU) on a modern video card. Checking several billion passwords per second is well within reach.[30]

Additionally, a dedicated password-cracking rig can achieve 350 billion passwords per second for Microsoft's LM hashing algorithm.[31]

Keep in mind that these two benchmarks describe the state of password cracking from 2013 and 2014, respectively. Cracking has only gotten faster since, due to Moore's Law. So the defense against this is to use Moore's Law to make defenses stronger over time. This is done with tunable password-hashing algorithms.

Tunable password-hashing algorithms can be thought of as carefully salted passwords that don't just get hashed once. Instead, the password P is hashed to produce hash $H1$. Then $H1$ is hashed to produce $H2$. This is repeated tens of thousands of times. So a defender can decide how much time they're willing to spend on password hashing at user login time. Something like a tenth of a second might be appropriate. The defender then works backward to see how many hashing iterations can fit in that amount of time. The login logic is then set up to hash that many times on each login. In approximately eighteen months, when Moore's Law has kicked in again and made it easier to do that hashing operation, the defender can double the number of hashing iterations and maintain the level of security they had at the outset. The tunable nature of this defense is key. As time goes on, the defender can keep adjusting the number of hashing iterations to provide the desired performance/cost tradeoff.

Password Storage Done Right

Remember how easy it was to get crypto wrong, even if you knew enough to use AES? It's nearly as easy to get hashing wrong. And, as is always the case with developing cryptographic software, the ways in which hashing goes wrong

---

30. https://security.stackexchange.com/questions/38134/what-are-realistic-rates-for-brute-force-hashing
31. https://arstechnica.com/information-technology/2012/12/25-gpu-cluster-cracks-every-standard-windows-password-in-6-hours/

tend not to be obvious errors that prevent themselves as bugs. They tend to show up as attacks that make researchers famous. So if you're looking at hashing passwords, you want to use a trustworthy implementation of one of the following algorithms:

1. bcrypt[32]

2. scrypt[33]

3. Argon2[34]

4. PBKDF2[35]

All of these are solid choices. All of these use salts correctly to prevent rainbow attacks and they're all tunably slow, so they're resistant to brute forcing and can become more so over time by adjusting their work factors. Earlier we covered criteria to evaluate cryptographic software even though we aren't elite cryptographers ourselves. All four of these hold up. They're well regarded, they've been well studied, and they were written by people with great track records.

Storing Passwords When You're the Client

So now we have four perfectly good password-hashing algorithms we can use. They're so good it's tempting to think that we've solved password storage for all use cases. Unfortunately, that's not the case. We can only use these for hashing the passwords of clients that authenticate to us. If we need to authenticate to another system, we can't use these password-hashing algorithms because they're one-way only. We can never get the passwords back from a hash. So we'll need another approach for storing passwords that we need to present to other systems.

Storing Passwords on Servers

How should we store passwords that are used by our servers to connect to other servers? Perhaps we could encrypt them before we store them on disk. That sounds good, but it doesn't buy us much. The problem is that the decryption key has to be available in the clear so that our application can decrypt the password in the config file at run time. So how do we protect that

---

32. https://en.wikipedia.org/wiki/Bcrypt
33. https://www.tarsnap.com/scrypt.html
34. https://password-hashing.net/#argon2
35. https://www.ietf.org/rfc/rfc2898.txt

decryption key? Eventually, our applications need to have access to credentials in the clear.

The applications we build need to have access to the secrets they require in the clear. Whenever possible, we should run each application on a dedicated server running as a dedicated service account. For example, use separate accounts for your web server and database server, and only give the database account access to the database server.

If we can't manage to put each application on a dedicated server, our only other option is to leverage OS permissions. We can use a separate OS account for each application that runs on a given server. This isn't a very strong defense because operating system privilege escalation vulnerabilities are discovered all the time. We should consider a compromise of any account on a server to compromise the entire server. But in situations where multiple applications have to run on a single server, this can at least be a speed bump that slows down an attacker.

It can be worthwhile to use a key store like Azure Key Vault, AWS Key Management Service, or HashiCorp Vault. They don't keep your secrets safer than not using them, since a compromise of a client of one of these key stores will result in compromised keys, just as would be the case if there were no key store in place. What the key stores provide is an audit trail of key access and key rotation. So by using these, you'll have an easier time determining which hosts accessed which keys and when. You'll also have a way to keep track of how often the keys have been rotated.

Storing Passwords on Workstations

When it comes to passwords on workstations that you use to authenticate to other systems, use a password manager such as 1Password. The biggest benefit of this is that you'll be able to use a separate password for every website you log into. This helps you because if one of the websites you use is compromised, the attackers won't be able to use your password from one website to give them access to other websites. The next benefit is that you'll be able to generate long passwords drawn from large alphabets. Password managers have fancy additional features like cloud-based sharing between devices. Only use these kinds of features if you must. Better to type them in by hand if you only have a couple passwords to share between devices. Password managers also have fancy browser plugins to streamline the pasting of passwords into login forms. It's better to not enable these and instead just copy and paste from 1Password. These plugins increase your attack surface but don't add very much usability.

Minimizing the Cost of Credential Loss

Credentials such as keys and passwords, by their nature, are extremely valuable to attackers and difficult to work with securely. Of course we do our best to keep them safe, but what if we fail? Is there anything we can do to soften the blow?

Consider this serious-looking equation:

Cost of Lost Credential == Likelihood of Loss x Value of Lost Credential

The rest of this book addresses the first term—lowering the likelihood of a successful attack. That's good; that's where we should focus most of our efforts. But we should prepare for the worst. Let's assume that some day, despite our best efforts, we lose control of our credentials. Since we can't 100% guarantee that we'll never lose credentials, we should take steps ahead of time to lower the cost of the loss by lowering the value of the credentials as much as possible.

We minimize the value of credentials in three main ways:

1. We limit the time in which a given credential is valid.

2. We limit the power of a user password by splitting authority between a password and a second factor.

3. We limit the scope in which a given credential can be used.

Limiting the Time a Credential Is Valid

The simplest way to decrease the value of a credential is to limit the time in which it is valid. No special security knowledge needed, just a bit of deployment savvy.

We get a double return on the effort invested into frequent rotation of credentials. Not only does this help lower the value of our credentials, this is also a capability we need to have in our system anyway. If we ever detect a compromise, we'll need to rotate all the affected credentials as part of the remediation. Better to have a frequently used, fully automated way to change them than to scramble and learn to do it in the aftermath of a breach. We also need to have the ability to rotate credentials when key members of our team leave the company. After someone leaves, we should rotate all the credentials they had access to.

Credentials used by programs to authenticate to other programs are great candidates for frequent rotation. Programs don't have problems remembering new credentials. And since programs can't use two-factor authorization (2FA) as an extra layer of protection around their credentials, it's good to use frequent rotation as an extra layer of protection.

If credentials never change, then an attacker who steals a credential once has access forever. With frequent credential rotation, an attacker who steals a credential once would either have to make frequent attacks to steal the new credentials or use the initial access to establish persistent access. Both of these make the attack noisier, which hopefully will lead to detection. Additionally, in time, the initial vulnerability may be fixed. Then, once credentials rotate, the attacker is locked out again.

Limiting the Power of a Credential with 2FA

Frequent rotation is great for credentials used by software but problematic for credentials used by people. People can't remember very many strong passwords and can have trouble remembering new passwords all the time. So when it comes to decreasing the value of passwords used by people, our best bet is to limit their value by splitting authority between a password and a second factor such as a two-factor authentication (2FA) system like YubiKey or Google Authenticator. With 2FA in place, the value of a stolen password is much lower. Additionally, login attempts that don't have a corresponding 2FA event make for a high-quality signal that an attack is underway. Monitor these if you can. We'll cover 2FA in more detail in *2FA*, on page 108.

Limiting the Scope of a Credential

Finally, we decrease the value of credentials by decreasing the scope on which they work. Instead of having one superpowerful system account with access to everything, try to have multiple, less-privileged accounts. That way, if one credential is compromised, it doesn't give over access to everything.

We saw one application of this principle back in *Layering Additional Defenses as a Mitigation Against Future Mistakes*, on page 34. We saw that splitting database access across multiple accounts can limit the impact of SQL injection and make attack attempts noisier.

Credentials with limited permissions aren't just for databases. This same principle can be applied to operating system permissions as well. A typical web application has a web server and a database. Prefer deployments where the database runs as a different user than the web server. Ideally, the database and the web server would be further separated onto different computers. And if there are scheduled tasks, say, in cron, each of them should run as a different user. That way if one of them is compromised, it won't provide a way for an attacker to move throughout the environment.

Similarly, for user accounts, grant permissions to people on a need-to-use basis only.

Keeping Passwords Hard to Predict

Passwords are meant to be secrets shared between a user and the server they're authenticating to. If attackers can predict those passwords, they can bypass this defense. Here are a couple steps we can take to keep it difficult for an attacker to predict a password.

Never Use Default Passwords

We covered this back in *Default Passwords*, on page 48, but it's worth mentioning again. Never use default passwords.

Monitor Password Dumps for Password Reuse

It's worthwhile to consider the ways credentials can be compromised. In general, it's much more likely for a password to be stolen from a server or phished than it is to be brute forced.

Brute forcing passwords through the front end of a web application is impractical. It's a noisy attack that can be stopped by account locking or by slowing down login attempts. Even if there is no automated defense, it's just slow. And brute forcing one account does nothing to speed up compromise of a second account.

A more likely attack is to try passwords from another compromised account. An attacker can compromise other sites or use passwords from password dumps from other compromised sites. Both of these sources give an attacker a combination of login/password pairs, so they can be very effective given how common password reuse is.

We can defend ourselves against this by monitoring published password dumps and see if any of our users' credentials are listed. You can set up your own monitoring system by searching online for password dumps. The specifics of where to look are likely to change over time, but at the time of this writing a good starting point is to search Pastebin for your users' email addresses.[36]

---

36. https://pastebin.com

Alternately, you can use a service such as Troy Hunt's "Have I Been Pwned?" to notify you when users from your domain show up in password dumps.[37]

Prevent Password Reuse Via Password Strength Requirements

A defense that's covered in more detail in the *Password Policy*, on page 87, Windows chapter is to require long passwords. It is unlikely that any of your users use long passwords elsewhere, so compromise of unrelated third-party websites is unlikely to impact you if you require long passwords. If users are security conscious enough to already be using long passwords on their personal accounts, they probably don't reuse passwords.

TLS Configuration

So far, the encryption we've discussed is for encryption at rest—that is, the encryption we use when storing or retrieving data. We also need to consider encryption in transit, the encryption used to protect data sent over the network. Just as we don't want to write our own crypto for encryption at rest, we shouldn't write our own crypto for encryption in transit. We use the same criteria we used earlier in this chapter—use a trustworthy implementation of well-researched algorithms. Today, the best candidate we have for encryption in transit is TLS 1.3. At the time of this writing, TLS 1.3 support isn't pervasive, however, so you may need to use TLS 1.2 in the short term. That's ok; properly configured TLS 1.2 is a strong choice as well. But going forward, your preference should be to use TLS 1.3 and only use TLS 1.2 if you depend on software that doesn't support TLS 1.3 yet.

We saw earlier that just because something is encrypted with AES doesn't mean it's encrypted securely. The same applies to TLS 1.2. There are a lot of configuration choices to be made in securely setting up TLS. If you want to learn all about the configuration choices to be made and how to make those choices, read Bulletproof SSL and TLS by Ivan Ristić.[38] If you're in a hurry and just want to know whether your server is well configured or not, check out the SSL Labs server test,[39] also from Ivan Ristić. The feedback from the SSL Labs site is quite clear and actionable. It will list common misconfigurations, such as weak cipher suites that are still supported by your servers. This site is kept up-to-date to reflect new research and attacks. Keep at it until you get an *A* from SSL Labs. Once you have a strong configuration, use that configuration throughout your organization.

---

37. https://haveibeenpwned.com/

38. https://www.feistyduck.com/books/bulletproof-ssl-and-tls/

39. https://www.ssllabs.com/

What's the Difference Between HTTPS, SSL, and TLS?

The terminology here is a little confusing. HTTP is the network protocol used to serve up web pages. Great protocol, but insecure because all of the communication is unencrypted. This was fine for allowing scientists to exchange research papers (the use case that Tim Berners-Lee initially had in mind when creating HTTP), but it's not safe enough for the many uses of the web today. So another protocol called HTTPS, or HTTP Secure, was invented. This encrypted the HTTP traffic before sending it out on the network. Early versions of HTTPS used a protocol called Secure Socket Layer (SSL) to encrypt the HTTP traffic. Versions 1, 2, and 3 of SSL were discovered to have security flaws. The replacement of SSL 3 was not called SSL 4, however. It was a new protocol called Transport Layer Security (TLS). TLS 1.0 and 1.1 have both been found to have flaws, and now we should use TLS 1.2 or TLS 1.3, except when legacy systems require us to use older protocols for backward compatibility.

These name changes haven't always taken hold in common usage. It's still common to hear people talk about websites protected by SSL, regardless of whether the underlying protocol is really SSL 2, SSL 3, TLS 1.0, TLS 1.1, TLS 1.2, or TLS 1.3.

Another aspect of secure TLS configuration is certificates. Certificates are stored on the HTTPS server and are used for a server to establish its identity. Read Bulletproof SSL and TLS for a more detailed explanation of how they work. For our purposes, let's think of them as files that are tied to private keys that need to be kept secure. Think back to our section on decreasing the value of the secrets we must keep. Since certificates and private keys are generated using cryptographically strong sources of randomness instead of easily remembered text, it's virtually impossible that an adversary would ever be able to compromise them via brute forcing. The more likely threat is that a private key would be compromised by gaining access to the server that uses it. So you will want to rotate your certificates at least annually. And you will want to be able to rotate them on short notice in the event your servers are compromised.

What's Next?

Cryptography is very difficult to get right. Don't write your own, and don't use low-level libraries either. Instead, use high-level libraries that have a degree of misuse-resistance. Use NaCl,[40] libsodium,[41] or Tink[42] for encryption at rest. Use TLS 1.3 (or TLS 1.2 if you have legacy constraints) in a configuration that gets an *A* from SSL Labs[43] for data in transit. Use scrypt,[44] bcrypt,[45] PBKDF2,[46] or Argon2[47] for password hashing.

Next up, we'll take a look at some best practices relating to Windows. In particular, we'll take a look at the way that Windows handles password hashing.

---

40. https://nacl.cr.yp.to/
41. https://libsodium.org/
42. https://github.com/google/tink
43. https://www.ssllabs.com/
44. https://www.tarsnap.com/scrypt
45. https://en.wikipedia.org/wiki/Bcrypt
46. https://en.wikipedia.org/wiki/PBKDF2
47. https://password-hashing.net/#argon2

CHAPTER 4

Windows

Odds are most of the computers where you work run Windows. So let's take a look at some security advice that's specific to Windows. Most of the advice in this chapter echoes more general advice from previous chapters, but we'll see a couple of Windows-specific applications of that advice. We'll also take a look at Mimikatz, a widely used tool for stealing Windows passwords, as well as some defenses against it.

Windows Users

We're going to start out with some foundational Windows concepts before we move into best practices. Let's start with users. There are two main types of interactive user accounts in Windows—administrators and standard users. Administrators are able to install software and make significant changes to the system. Standard users don't have these permissions but are able to run installed software.

There is one other kind of user, but it's not an interactive user. It's called SYSTEM and it's the user that does work on behalf of Windows itself. Because it works on behalf of the operating system, it has complete permissions to everything on that computer. We'll come back to this a little later in the chapter.

When you have more than a handful of computers on your network, you'll want some things to be centrally controlled and managed. These would be things like user definition and user credentials (hashed passwords, not plaintext passwords as we saw in *Password Storage*, on page 70). In a Windows network, this grouping of computers along with its centralized control systems is called a domain. Users can be defined either on a domain, which means they can log in on computers throughout the domain, or they can be defined locally, which means they can only log in on the one computer they're defined on.

Login and Mimikatz

Let's take a look at what happens when a user logs in. How does Windows know that you are who you say you are? You supply a password. But how does Windows know that it's the right password? We saw in the cryptography chapter that systems that need to authenticate users should store password hashes, not the passwords themselves. Sure enough, Windows stores user password hashes, not the passwords themselves. Windows does this using a hashing algorithm called NTLM. Windows uses NTLM to generate a hash of the password that the user supplies at login time and compares it to the hash that's been stored for that user. If it's a local account, the known-good hash is stored on that computer. If it's a domain account, then the computer will ask the domain controller whether the supplied hash is the right one.

When else is the password needed?

It's needed when you access domain resources like shared drives. It would be awkward if you had to type in your password every time you accessed any domain resource. So Windows keeps your password hash in memory and sends it whenever you need to access domain resources. The domain controller verifies the password hash; and if it matches, the domain controller grants access. This makes for a smooth user experience. But are there security implications? Well, one implication is that the password hash has to remain in memory. That implication is the basis for a tool called Mimikatz.[1]

Mimikatz is a tool that reads the password hashes that Windows keeps in memory. Due to the way that Windows stores these passwords, any user with administrator-level access to a Windows computer can read the password hashes of any other users that are logged in at the same time. And in earlier versions of Windows, such as Windows 7 and Windows 8.1, Mimikatz could also read the plaintext passwords of any logged-in users.

Let's think about what a tool like Mimikatz enables an attacker to do. Let's say that an attacker can execute code as a local admin on a Windows computer on a network. This capability might come from stolen credentials or from a software vulnerability. The attacker can then run Mimikatz and get the password hashes of any other users who are logged in. If any of those users are domain users, then the attacker can run commands as those users

---

1. https://github.com/gentilkiwi/mimikatz

on other machines in the domain using the Pass the Hash attack. And if any of those users are local admins on the other computers, then the attacker can run Mimikatz on that second population of computers and possibly steal more password hashes and expand out to another set of computers. If any of these computers have domain admins logged in, then the attacker can steal domain admin password hashes, which generally results in complete compromise of the domain.

Joe asks:
What Is the Pass the Hash Attack?

We've seen that Windows keeps user password hashes in memory to allow a logged-in user to access domain resources. Windows allows users to authenticate themselves to remote Windows computers by sending a valid password hash over TCP port 445, which is the SMB port. So if a password hash is stolen with Mimikatz, the attacker can use that hash to impersonate the users on other computers. This is the Pass the Hash attack.

For a more detailed explanation, see Pass-the-hash attacks: Tools and Mitigation by Ewaida and Boeynaems.[a]

---

a.   www.sans.org/reading-room/whitepapers/testing/pass-the-hash-attacks-tools-mitigation-33283

It's worth noting that while Mimikatz makes it easier to accomplish this attack, the underlying problem would be there regardless of whether Mimikatz existed or not. If Mimikatz did not exist, it would be necessary to invent it.

So how do we prevent this attack on our network?

We have a number of defenses available to us, the first of which is to keep up-to-date on patching. As long as we're on Windows 8.1 or newer, Mimikatz should only be able to steal password hashes, not passwords themselves. In the chapter on patching, we focused on incremental security bug fixes as the main benefit to keeping up-to-date on patches. But there are also systemic improvements like this one. There is a registry setting that would make Windows store the actual passwords, not just the hashes, in memory. But you won't have this enabled by default. And as your security posture improves, you'll add endpoint monitoring to prevent settings like this from being enabled or to at least warn you if they're changed.

Another defense against Mimikatz is better network segmentation. The workstations on your network should not generally need to communicate with each other via SMB on port 445. So block that at the router level. Then, even if one workstation is compromised, the attacker won't be able to jump from workstation to workstation looking for one with logged-in domain admins. There's still need for domain administrators to use port 445 to administer machines on your network, so you'll want to enable port 445 for communication initiated by admins; just block port 445 for communication initiated by other computers.

Since the attacker's target is domain admin credentials, make those credentials harder to find by using them less often. If the domain admin credentials are only used when they're absolutely needed, fewer machines will have domain admin credentials in memory and for shorter periods of time. This also provides a layer of defense against phishing. Domain admins aren't immune to phishing attacks. If they always use their regular domain user to check email, then even if they get phished, they'll only provide a regular domain account, not a domain admin account.

This gives us three different levels of access that administrators in your organization will need to have:

- Regular domain user for doing their day-to-day work, reading email, and so on

- Domain admin user for doing work that requires domain admin access, things like editing domain policies

- Local admin on other people's workstations for administration and troubleshooting purposes

So you'll want your domain administrators to use a separate account for each of these three access levels. The first two are straightforward, but a couple of other options are available for the third account.

One option for domain administrators who need local administrator access to workstations for troubleshooting and support is to use Microsoft's Local Administrator Password Solution, or LAPS.[2] The idea behind LAPS is that it manages the local administrator account on each machine in the domain for you. So each machine has a unique local administrator password. So even if the local administrator's password hash (or even the password itself) on one computer is compromised, the attacker can't use it on any other computer. The other nice thing it does is automatically rotate the local administrator passwords, which minimizes the impact of a stolen local administrator password.

---

2.   https://technet.microsoft.com/en-us/mt227395.aspx

Another approach is to create a local admins group in Active Directory. Then put that group in the Local Administrators group on each workstation in your organization. Make this a part of your standard workstation image.

Password Policy

It's a good idea to set a Windows policy that requires a long password for domain accounts. There are two main reasons for this. The first is the math of cracking passwords given an NTLM password hash. In contrast to the recommended password hashing algorithms that we saw in *Password Storage Done Right*, on page 74 (bcrypt, scrypt, Argon2, and PBKDF2), the NTLM password hashing algorithm does not have a work factor associated with it. This means that an attacker who gets access to an NTLM password hash will be able to attempt to brute force it with a huge number of attempts per second. The NTLM algorithm is not going away any time soon. So our only other defense against this attack is to use a longer password.

Another benefit from longer passwords relates to password storage from a long time ago. Before NTLM, Windows used a password hashing algorithm called LM. LM hashing hasn't aged well and is quite susceptible to brute forcing. Because of this, exposing an LM hash to an attacker (via Mimikatz, for example) should be considered equivalent to exposing a password to an attacker. The reason this affects us is that Windows servers can be configured to store both the NTLM password hash as well as the LM password hash for reasons of backward compatibility. Your domain should be configured to only use NTLM hashes, but you can buy some cheap insurance against getting that wrong. LM hashing only works on passwords that are 14 characters or shorter. So if you require passwords that are 15 characters or longer, you won't be able to make the mistake of allowing LM hashes.

For more details on preventing usage of LM passwords, see Microsoft's How to Prevent Windows from Storing a LAN Manager Hash of Your Password in Active Directory and Local SAM Databases.[3]

One more, often overlooked, advantage of requiring a long domain password is that your users probably don't use that password anywhere else. When large password breaches make the news, you have to worry about your users reusing passwords from that account at work. You can buy yourself some peace of mind by requiring a long password for your domain. It's unlikely that any of your users will have chosen long passwords for themselves if they

---

3. https://support.microsoft.com/en-us/help/299656/how-to-prevent-windows-from-storing-a-lan-manager-hash-of-your-passwor

didn't have to. If they were security conscious enough to choose a long pass-word for their personal use, they'd likely be security conscious enough to not reuse passwords. So you're unlikely to be impacted by external password leaks.

Putting all this together, we have a pretty good basis for choosing a minimum password policy of 15–20 characters. It's worth noting that the minimum password length in Windows maxes out at 14. This is due to backward com-patibility with the LM password-hashing algorithm. So if you want this to be enforced via technical means instead of just having it written down as com-pany policy, you'll need to have your users change passwords via another tool where you can enforce the longer password length. One such tool is Okta. Okta is a Single Sign-On solution for coordinating user access to online tools. Once installed, it can be used to handle user password resets and can enforce a minimum password requirement longer than 14 characters. Two more benefits of pervasive use of Single Sign-On are that you can use it to require 2FA for all your internal web apps, and you'll have a single place to disable access to all internal websites when someone leaves your organization.

The last piece of a password rotation policy is password rotation frequency. Both GCHQ[4] and NIST[5] have recently released guidance about passwords. The takeaway that you're likely to hear about is that these two organizations no longer call for enforcing regularly scheduled user password rotation. What may get glossed over is that as a part of shifting the burden for effective password usage from users to site operators, they make additional suggestions, including the following:

- Enable a rate-limiting mechanism that effectively limits the number of failed authentication attempts that can be made on the subscriber's account.

- Add support for all printable characters in passwords.

- Prevent users from using passwords known to be commonly used, expected, or compromised. Examples of such passwords include:
  - Passwords obtained from previous breach corpuses
  - Dictionary words
  - Repetitive or sequential characters (such as 'aaaaaa' and '1234abcd')
  - Context-specific words, such as the name of the service, the username, and derivatives thereof

---

4.   https://www.ncsc.gov.uk/guidance/password-guidance-simplifying-your-approach
5.   https://pages.nist.gov/800-63-3/

- Don't provide password hints.

- Don't allow for knowledge-based questions that come from publicly available data (ex: mother's maiden name or name of childhood friend) as part of handling a password reset.

- If 2FA is supported, provide at least one 2FA option that doesn't use the public phone network.

And of course, passwords should be rotated if there is reason to believe they've been compromised.

If you require passwords of at least 15 characters for your Windows logins, you're pretty well on your way to meeting these requirements. You don't have explicit support for preventing the weak passwords that NIST describes, but the password length is a decent approximation. Add in a subscription to a compromised password service like Have I Been Pwned,[6] and you'll be in pretty good shape for not requiring regularly scheduled user password rotation.

Active Directory: What Else Is It Good For?

We need to maintain Active Directory in order to run a Windows domain. Can we leverage that investment and get any other benefits from it? It turns out that we can. One of the best of these is the ability to disable access in a single place when someone leaves our organization or we learn that their account has been compromised.

Consider this scenario: A popular social networking site announces that it has suffered a massive security breach, and a copy of the account names and passwords for all of its users is now floating around the internet. You happen to discuss this with one of your coworkers, who mentions that they're a little worried because they use that site and they've used that same password on a number of work-related websites. How do you lock down access?

It's hard to respond to an external breach like this if you don't have a single place to turn off access. You'd have to work on

(number of work-related websites) x (number of people in your organization)

different accounts. This is probably too many accounts to track down. But if you had all access go through a single system, you could cut off all access there and work with each user affected by the external breach to reestablish access. Active Directory can be that single system.

---

6.   https://haveibeenpwned.com/

Similarly, how do you disable access for employees who leave the company? If you have to wade through a large number of systems each time someone leaves the company, you leave the door open for user error that could leave accounts active long past the time when the employee left. In this case also, you're much better off having access go through Active Directory.

In both of these cases, we see problems that arise from having a single, highly valuable store of hashed passwords. If that store of hashed passwords is compromised, whether through direct access to the password hashes, password reuse, or the memory of a disgruntled former employee, you have a big problem on your hands. How can we decrease the value of these credentials? One approach is to introduce two-factor authorization. We talked briefly about 2FA back in the Crypto chapter. Let's get into a little more detail here.

When you set up a system to use 2FA for access, you split access between a password that the user remembers and a second, very short-lived password that an external device such as a smartphone app can generate on demand. Someone who only has one of these factors can't access the system without the other. With a system like this in place, even if a user's password is leaked due to password reuse with third-party systems, the attacker won't be able to log in because they won't have access to the 2FA app, which generates the other part of the login credentials. What's more, 2FA makes attempts to use stolen passwords much noisier and more noticeable. If an attacker attempts to log in with a valid username and password but doesn't have the 2FA app, this should stand out in your logs. It is rare for a user to enter their credentials but not complete the login process by using their 2FA application. If you see this happen, especially if the attempt originates from an IP address that's not typically used by the legitimate user, you have a very strong indication that the password has been compromised and should be rotated.

BitLocker

BitLocker is Microsoft's full disk encryption (FDE) solution. It encrypts the entire file system transparently to the user and the applications. This is a defense against attackers with physical access, but since the file system is decrypted automatically once the system boots up, this doesn't provide any defense against malware or attackers with access to the machine via stolen creds or that are exploiting vulnerable software running on the box.

Without an FDE solution in place, an attacker with physical access can just pull the hard drive out of the victim's computer, copy it to an external drive, and take the external drive away for investigation. While an attacker has the hard drive removed from the computer, they can also attach it to a computer owned by the attacker, copy malware onto the victim's hard drive, then put the hard drive back in the victim's computer. Additionally, an attacker can carry out the "Sticky Keys attack." The Sticky Keys attack has been known since at least 2009, but there doesn't appear to be a definitive attribution for it.

Sticky Keys Attack

The Sticky Keys functionality is an accessibility feature of Windows. It allows people who can't physically press multiple keys on a keyboard at once to interact with their keyboard as though they could. One of the most common uses of this is to make use of the Shift key more accessible. Instead of requiring a user to physically press both the Shift key and a letter key at the same time in order to make a capital letter, when Sticky Keys is enabled, the system considers the Shift key to be held down until it is pressed a second time. It means more key strokes, but none of them have to happen at the same time. In Windows, a small program called c:\windows\system32\sethc.exe configures whether or not Sticky Keys is enabled for the user currently logged in. The user runs this program by hitting the Shift key five times in a row.

It's nice that this feature exists, but why do we care about esoteric accessibility features in a security book?

We care because c:\windows\system32\sethc.exe runs as the SYSTEM user, not a regular user. You can trigger Sticky Keys for use during the login process, before you've authenticated yourself. Because it runs before login, it can't run as a regular user; the computer doesn't know who you are yet. We can combine this with a lack of full disk encryption to launch the Sticky Keys attack.

The Sticky Keys attack assumes an attacker has physical access to a Windows workstation. To perform the attack, the attacker powers down the workstation and boots up via a bootable device such as a USB drive that contains a small bootable Linux disk image. Once the system has booted up into Linux, the attacker overwrites c:\windows\system32\sethc.exe with a copy of c:\windows\system32\cmd.exe. (Recall that running cmd.exe is the same as opening a new Command Prompt window.) Then the attacker reboots normally into Windows. When the attacker sees the login screen, the attacker hits Shift five times. When this happens, Windows thinks that the user wants to configure the Sticky Keys settings, and so it runs c:\windows\system32\sethc.exe. But the attacker has previously overwritten this file with c:\windows\system32\cmd.exe! So Windows will present the attacker with a Command Prompt running as the SYSTEM user. This attacker has full control of the machine at this point and can install or run any software they want. The attacker also has full control of the registry and the file system.

These two attacks illustrate the problems that arise when a computer's hard drive is accessible to an attacker with physical access when the computer is powered down. When an attacker bypasses the operating system's permissions by accessing the hard drive directly, the attacker is able to launch significant attacks.

The defense against these attacks is full disk encryption. When full disk encryption is enabled, the attacker is no longer able to bypass the operating system's defenses. Until the operating system boots, the file system is encrypted, and an attacker cannot trivially read from or write to the hard drive.

What's Next?

We've covered some of the basic Windows defenses we should have in place. We've also seen how some of the more generic advice from earlier in the book (patch as soon as possible, make attacks noisier) shows up again in this chapter.

What can an attacker do if all these defenses are in place? Bypass them. We'll take a look at phishing and what to do about it in our next chapter.

Beware geeks bearing emails.

    Adapted from The Aeneid

CHAPTER 5

Phishing

Phishing is the first attack we've covered that attacks the user instead of the software. In a phishing attack, the attacker sends an email to the victim and tricks the victim into doing something the attacker wants them to do—generally, reveal their login credentials. Once an attacker has the victim's credentials, they are no longer impeded by the defenses that we've carefully built up over the previous chapters. No need for an attacker to look for unpatched servers, weak cryptography, or SQL injection if they can just log in and use the system as a legitimate user. It sounds simple, and it is technologically simpler than the attacks we've covered so far, but there's no prize for complexity. Phishing continues to be a problem because it continues to be effective.

Types of Phishing Attacks

Phishers don't need to trick everyone they email in order to be successful. They generally cast a wide net and count on someone to have an off day and go along with the attack. Duo's *The Trouble With Phishing* states that 17% of people who receive phishing emails enter their credentials into phishing sites.[1] Put another way, on average, a phisher with just six email addresses can expect to trick one of the account owners into revealing their login credentials.

It's just an email. What's the worst that could happen? Let's take a look at the most common types of phishing attacks.

Phished Credentials

By far, the most common phishing attack is to steal login credentials. Generally this is done by setting up a malicious website that looks the same as the login screen for Gmail, Outlook 365, Dropbox, or another popular website.

---

1.   https://duo.com/resources/ebooks/the-trouble-with-phishing

The phisher then sends a phishing email to the intended victim. The phishing email will contain a link to the malicious website as part of a message that claims that it's important for the recipient to click on the link and log in. If the phisher is "lucky," Pavlovian conditioning will kick in when the user sees what appears to be a familiar login screen and the user will submit their credentials to the malicious website.

Stolen credentials can be quite damaging. A phisher who has taken over an email account can probably trigger password resets for most of the other online services associated with that email address, like social media accounts and financial accounts. The phisher can exfiltrate old email. If the phisher wants to take over the account, in general, they can reset the password for the email account to lock the victim out of the account. If the phisher wants to be stealthier, they can use the newly compromised email account to send further phishing emails to people in the compromised account's address book and then delete them from the account to make it harder for the legitimate account owner to discover. These phishing emails will have added credibility because the new wave of victims will see the email as having been sent by someone they know. This credibility increases the likelihood that the recipient will click on the link and follow instructions to log in.

What do phishing emails look like? Many phishing emails are generic and are meant to be sent out widely. A common premise for these is the past-due invoice. These phishing emails create a sense of urgency by claiming that the victim is behind on payments and will get in trouble if they don't pay right away. When these phishing emails are successful, the phisher will use the newly acquired credentials to resend the phishing email to people in the new victim's contact list and continue the process. But a phisher who has a specific target in mind can tailor the phishing email. After doing research about the company, an attacker can forge an email that, at first glance, appears to come from an important executive, customer, or vendor. The subject could pertain to recent company events. Phishing emails could be sent out in batches to see what gets the best responses in order to tweak later batches. Early waves of reconnaissance emails could be used to look for common email signatures or terminology that's in use at the company.

XSRF

If we think back to a section in the Vulnerabilities chapter, *Cross-Site Request Forgery (XSRF)*, on page 40, we see another attack vector for the successful phisher—XSRF. Recall what an XSRF vulnerability on foo.com allows an attacker to do. It allows an attacker to target logged-in users of foo.com and get them to take whatever actions on foo.com the attacker wants them to. All the attacker needs to do is to get them to visit a URL that the attacker controls. Phishing is a great way for an attacker to get a victim to visit a URL that the attacker controls.

Put another way, if you're logged in to your bank's website and the bank's website doesn't defend against XSRF, and then you click on a link in a phishing email, the phisher can take over your browser to interact with the bank's website. This includes transferring money, changing passwords, changing contact information, or anything else you'd be able to do while logged in.

If you're building a website or a web app, then it's important for you to prevent XSRF attacks in your site. If your site is vulnerable to XSRF, then if someone's logged in to your app while also reading email, there's a clear path for attackers to take over your web app—they just email people who are logged in.

This attack is more tailored and a lot more work for the phisher, so you're much less likely to encounter this in practice.

Social Engineering

Social engineering is a less technical type of attack. In this kind of attack, a phisher would pretend to be someone they're not and ask for things they shouldn't have—HR records, banking information, passwords, and so on. This kind of attack is different because it probably won't contain a link to a malicious or XSRF-vulnerable website. It probably just comes out and asks the intended victim to do something on behalf of the phisher.

Malware

Malware-based phishing emails are the least likely attack. It's comparatively hard to write custom malware to attack phishing victims. Most of the time phishers are just after credentials anyway. And the odds of stealing credentials are so high that it's generally not worth the effort to try to develop custom malware. Most phishers just increase their chances for success by sending out more phishing emails.

There are two kinds of malware-based phishing attacks. By far the most common is the phishing email that contains a malware attachment and a pretense for why the recipient should execute the attachment. Generally these are just Microsoft Office documents with embedded macros that open a credential harvesting website. They tend not to be sophisticated. These can be avoided with proper training. The other kind of malware-based phishing attack is the one that attacks the email client itself. It is difficult to find vulnerabilities in email clients, so writing malware that targets vulnerabilities in specific mail clients is expensive, time-consuming, and only viable against users of specific mail clients. Because of this, phishing that targets mail clients is very rare and generally only attempted by sophisticated attackers like nation states. For a funny take on the difference between nation state attackers and everyone else, take a look at James Mickens's hilarious "This World of Ours."[2] It's not the most actionable essay I link to in this book, but it's definitely the funniest.

Whatever the specifics of malware delivery, a phisher can do lots of bad things with the ability to run a custom program on a victim's computer. Common choices include keyloggers, remote monitoring tools, remote administration tools, and credential-stealing software.

Social Defense

You'll want to provide training for the people in your organization so they develop a healthy level of skepticism toward incoming email. You can put the training together yourself or hire an outside firm. Your best defense is vigilant colleagues. Most phishing attacks spread a wide net, so increasing the likelihood that even one person notices the deception allows you to respond and get the word out sooner. We'll cover phishing responses later in this chapter.

Here are the basic points you'll want to emphasize in your anti-phishing training.

- Don't embarrass your colleagues.
- Be extra skeptical about emails with urgent deadlines.
- Be suspicious of strange-looking domains in links and email addresses.
- Be skeptical about attachments.
- Consider whether the premise of the email makes sense.

Let's look at each of these points.

First, you need to make sure that if people get phished they'll feel safe enough to report that right away. People won't feel safe if they're teased or blamed for getting phished. They won't feel safe if they see those things happen to someone else, either. The sooner you find out that someone handed over their credentials, the less damage there will be. If your colleagues are worried that they'll get in trouble for coming forward and announcing that they got phished, they are more likely to just clam up and hope the whole thing blows over without telling anyone.

---

2.   https://www.usenix.org/system/files/1401_08-12_mickens.pdf

A trait common to many phishing emails is a sense of urgency to get the victim to act quickly. One example of this is a phishing email that was forged to appear to be sent by a company executive who needs help handling an important customer request right away. Another example is a phishing email that pretends to be from a vendor who hasn't been paid for an invoice and needs payment right away. These are just pretenses to get the recipient to act quickly without thinking through what they're doing or what websites they're entering their password into.

Another trait that is common to phishing emails is that they are often forged to look like they were sent from someone legitimate. Email uses several headers related to the identity of the sender, including From and Reply To. Be suspicious when these headers don't all match. Also, be aware when the domains in use in these fields are not familiar. Phishers will sometimes register new domains that look like legitimate domains and send emails from these domains. Examples of this would be registering a domain like fo0.com (the second letter *o* is replaced with a zero) and sending an email from ceo@fo0.com when trying to phish people at foo.com. These doppelgänger domains can also be used in links in the email. So remind colleagues to be suspicious of doppelgänger domains in the email headers and in links within the email.

Remind your colleagues to be suspicious of the links in an email. If an email claims to link to a shared document on outlook365.com, but the actual link points to sites like outl00k365.com, outlook356.somefilesharingservice.com, outlooook365.com, or ou.tlook365.com, be careful. This type of domain name is often a sign that the email is fraudulent.

Encourage your colleagues to go with their gut when reading email. Does the email "feel" right? Set aside all the technology. Does the premise of the email make sense? If an email is asking you to take urgent action to address an unpaid vendor but your role in your company doesn't have you interacting with vendors, then slow down and think about whether this email is legitimate. If the email claims to be from an important executive who needs your help right away but that executive has never asked you for this kind of help, seek independent verification of the email.

It is important to be skeptical about attachments. Don't open any attachment unless you were already expecting an attachment from the sender. If you must open an attachment, be sure that the file extension of the attached file is appropriate for the kind of attachment you're expecting. For instance, if you're expecting to receive a jpg image from someone, be sure that the file name ends in ".jpg" or ".jpeg", not ".jpg.exe". A file with a name ending in ".exe" is generally a program, not a picture. So if you download an ".exe" file and double-click on it, the phisher's program will run on your computer. Finally, if you must open Microsoft Office documents from an email, be sure to disable macros in Microsoft Office before opening the document.

If there is any question about the legitimacy of an email, verify the claims of the email without using the links in the email. In particular, don't trust links that ask you to log in to something. If the email claims to link to a shared document but the link presents you with a login screen, don't log in using that link. Instead, log into the file-sharing service as you normally would, then use the search capabilities of that file-sharing service to find the files that allegedly require your attention. If the email is legitimate, you'll find them. Similarly, if the email claims to be from someone at your company but something just feels off about it, walk over to their desk and ask if they really sent it.

Whatever training you decide on, be sure to make that training part of your onboarding process for new employees. Training isn't a one-time event; it has to keep up with the growth of your organization. Also be sure to offer refresher courses to staff who've been with the organization for a while. This will help keep everyone vigilant and keep everyone up-to-date on recent changes in the phishing landscape.

You'll want to run test phishing campaigns against your organization to help illustrate the importance of not clicking on links. One tool that can be useful in this is Gophish,[3] an open source phishing campaign tool. It's important to do this in a way that won't erode the relationship with the rest of the company. You'll want to announce that periodic phishing campaigns are part of the security posture of your organization. You'll want to have some kind of refresher training or readings for people who fall for the phishing email, but it's important to not single them out or embarrass them. Expect people to have questions and be glad for their interest.

It's good to develop the capabilities to investigate phishing emails. Keeping up with incoming phishing emails can quickly turn into a full-time job, though. So you'll probably only be able to investigate a small percentage of them. Even if you don't have the capacity to investigate them all, it's still worthwhile to train your organization to forward them all to a queue for investigation. First, this reinforces the anti-phishing training you'll want to give to your organization. Second, this will serve as a good record of what attacks have been attempted if you do have an incident.

---

3.   https://getgophish.com/documentation/

Don't DIY

Before we get into DNS-based defenses, here's a simple piece of advice about email hosting—don't do it yourself. Just host your company's email with [G Suite from Google.](https://gsuite.google.com/) (Ok, you could also pick Outlook 365 if you like Microsoft. There are other email hosting options, but I don't believe any of them are able to put as many resources into security as these two companies do.) It's a lot of work just to keep a mail server up and running with the reliability that email requires. It's even more work to keep it patched and configured securely. Maintaining a mail server is a full-time job. And if you want support on holidays, weekends, evenings, and sick days, it's a full-time job for more than one person. If your organization is just starting out, you have much better ways to use your employees' time than maintaining a mail server. Even if you've grown to 200 employees and use Google's most expensive hosting plan, you'd still spend less on G Suite than the cost of a single US-based full-time engineer. All three of the DNS tools we'll cover work with G Suite but aren't enabled out of the box. It's pretty straightforward to enable them as long as you have permissions to edit DNS records for your domain. G Suite maintains good documentation on all three of these tools.

DNS-Based Defense

We're going to look at three different DNS-based defenses for preventing anyone from forging email that looks like it came from your domain. It will be useful to be able to query DNS records to understand these defenses and configure them for your domains. If you're running a Unix-like operating system like Mac OS or Linux, you'll have a program called dig installed. You can run dig at the command line. You can read the man page for more details, but for our purposes all you need to know is to run dig with two arguments—the host or domain you want to learn more about and the keyword *txt*. That will look like this:

```
$ dig punkgrok.org txt

; <<>> DiG 9.8.3-P1 <<>> punkgrok.org txt
;; global options: +cmd
;; Got answer:
;; ->>HEADER<<- opcode: QUERY, status: NOERROR, id: 61669
;; flags: qr rd ra; QUERY: 1, ANSWER: 1, AUTHORITY: 3, ADDITIONAL: 3

;; QUESTION SECTION:
;punkgrok.org.                  IN      TXT

;; ANSWER SECTION:
punkgrok.org.          13492  IN      TXT
   "v=spf1 include:_spf.google.com -all
```

```
;; AUTHORITY SECTION:
punkgrok.org.           85485   IN      NS      ns3.dreamhost.com.
punkgrok.org.           85485   IN      NS      ns2.dreamhost.com.
punkgrok.org.           85485   IN      NS      ns1.dreamhost.com.

;; ADDITIONAL SECTION:
ns1.dreamhost.com.      121401  IN      A       64.90.62.230
ns2.dreamhost.com.      121401  IN      A       208.97.182.10
ns3.dreamhost.com.      121401  IN      A       66.33.205.230

;; Query time: 413 msec
;; SERVER: 192.168.43.1#53(192.168.43.1)
;; WHEN: Sat Jun 23 09:42:32 2018
;; MSG SIZE  rcvd: 193
```

If you don't have this tool available, there may be online equivalent tools. At the time of this writing, Google maintains a a web-based equivalent of the Unix dig command.[4]

The Problem with Email

Phishing emails that appear to have been sent from your domain are going to be more effective than phishing emails sent from other domains. So we're going to take a look at three technologies that you can use to help prevent phishers forging emails that appear to be sent from your domain—SPF, DKIM, and DMARC.

First let's look at a problem with email. Email is sent using a protocol called SMTP, or Simple Mail Transfer Protocol. SMTP is the protocol that allows mail servers from all over the internet to send email to one another. It's too complex to cover in detail here. What we'll emphasize here is that SMTP lets anyone send email from any address. That's problematic, and it's part of why there's so much spam.

Let's suppose, as we often do, that Alice wants to email Bob. When bob.com receives an incoming email claiming to be from alice@alice.com, there's nothing in SMTP that lets the bob.com mail server determine whether this email is legitimate or not. No matter what authentication is in place on the legitimate alice.com SMTP server, anyone can connect to bob.com's SMTP server and claim to be sending legitimate email from alice.com.

Solving this requires answering some tricky questions about identity. Who is bob.com to say who can and can't send email from alice.com addresses? Turns out that we already have a robust system for distributing authoritative

---

4. https://toolbox.googleapps.com/apps/dig/

information about domains. That system is the Domain Name System (DNS). We can leverage that system to narrow the scope of fraudulent emails.

The DNS system maintains records for all of the domains on the internet. DNS supports multiple record types. The first record type most people think of is the *A* record type. This is what lets us use a convenient machine name like www.pragprog.com instead of having to remember an IP address like 54.243.36.130. But there are other record types as well. One of these types is the TXT record type. TXT record types are meant for associating textual data with a domain. Generally TXT records are meant to be parsed by programs, rather than read by humans. As we'll see with SPF, DKIM, and DMARC, we can use the ability to store a little bit of data in a trusted, authoritative location like a DNS record to help bob.com answer the difficult question of whether incoming email from alice.com is legitimate. Adding these DNS-based defenses will keep phishers from being able to forge emails that appear to come from your domain. This will help both the people in your organization and in organizations that you regularly collaborate with.

SPF

Sender Policy Framework (SPF) is a technology that enables the administrators of a domain to specify which computers are authorized to send email on behalf of that domain. SPF leverages the Domain Name System (DNS) to distribute this information. This lets a mail server determine whether incoming email is legitimate. If incoming mail claims to have been sent from foo.com, the mail server that receives it can look at the DNS records for foo.com and see if the computer that's sending it the email is on the list of approved computers.

Going back to our example, if alice.com specifies an SPF record like this:

```
"v=spf1 ip4:1.2.3.4 -all"
```

then when bob.com receives an email that claims to be from alice@alice.com, bob.com has a way to determine its authenticity. If it's 1.2.3.4 that's connecting to bob.com to send the email, then it's legitimate. If it was sent by any other IP address, it's a forgery.

Specifying a single IP address is the simplest example to understand, but it's not very flexible. Fortunately, SPF gives us a couple other options for additional flexibility. Instead of just being able to specify a single IP address, SPF lets us specify multiple IPs and/or multiple CIDR blocks. If you need a refresher on CIDR, refer to *What Is a CIDR Range?*, on page 13. SPR also lets us defer to the SPF decisions of other computers. This is a key to using SPF with a hosted email solution like Gmail or Outlook 365. Looking back to the dig output for punkgrok.org, we can see that I've delegated SPF decisions to _spf.google.com because I use Gmail to handle all my mail at punkgrok.org.

The last part of the SPF record for us to investigate is the -all at the end of the line. This is how SPF lets us specify what to do when an email is received from an unapproved computer. The two most common options are -all, which is a hard fail, and ~all, which is a soft fail. An email that hard fails should not be presented to the end user. An email that soft fails should be presented to the end user, but with a warning that it might be spam.

There are more options to SPF configuration, but we've covered the parts you're most likely to want to use. For more details, see the SPF Project[5] or RFC 7208.[6]

DKIM

DomainKeys Identified Mail (DKIM) lets us lock down who can send email for our domain via cryptography. It can be used in addition to SPF. When we set up a domain to use DKIM, we add a public key to the DNS records for our domain, and then our mail server uses the corresponding private key to sign our outgoing emails. That way, when the mail server at another domain receives an email claiming to be from our domain, that mail server can look up our public key in DNS and verify that the signature on the email is legitimate.

Let's look at how that would play out in our example with Alice and Bob.

Alice wants legitimate emails from her domain, alice.com, to be trusted by other mail servers. With DKIM she can create a public/private key pair for this purpose. She'll keep the private key on her mail server. She'll make the public key available as a TXT record for a specific subdomain. Then, when she authenticates to her mail server to send an email to Bob, her mail server will sign the email using the private key. A signed email would have a special DKIM header that would look something like this:

```
DKIM-Signature: v=1; a=rsa-sha256; c=relaxed/relaxed;
d=alice.com; s=aliceselector;
h=From:Date:Subject:Message-ID:Content-Type:MIME-Version;
bh=f73482ef2e21c2cd80ce08ccb5030ec09eebc18562d=;
b=3I9lx/9QT8R2yJC5MmmUcZCYlP84iEhUmT0yvO4BXpsNP9yul5c7mNpF9SbZL8nFw+
chJCVOzrksZwajB95tGSaw7JXzctDBK+oj/pj2x2MFDi46cXYJ7N/6yh9CHHUI9NeFZ1
rtdAuXiNIZ9nofNvlUtTnNouWOcEi6fRSXrb8=
```

5.   http://www.openspf.org/
6.   https://tools.ietf.org/html/rfc7208

\|//
%
Joe asks:
How Do Signatures Prevent Forged Email?

Alice wants to send out messages and prove that they came from her. Public key signatures give her a way to do that.

First, Alice creates a public/private key pair. She keeps the private key private but distributes the public key far and wide via DNS. These keys are just really big numbers, hundreds of digits long. But these numbers aren't chosen at random. There's a mathematical relationship between them. The relationship between the private and public keys allows for some pretty interesting things:

- Alice can write a message and use the private key to create a signature for the message.

- Bob can look at the message, the signature, and the public key and then harness the power of math to prove that the signature was created by someone who had the private key. If Bob trusts that no one copied the private key from Alice, then Bob knows that Alice wrote the message.

- Eve can't figure out the private key even if she sees the message, the signature, and the public key.

This just describes what the signatures make possible. If you'd like to read more about the math behind this, read the excellent descriptions in either *Serious Cryptography*, *Cryptography Engineering*, or crypto101.io.

At first glance, this bunch of gibberish might not inspire a lot of faith. But this actually gives bob.com a lot of information to use to validate the incoming email. Let's go through each of the tags in this header.

- v=1; This just tells bob.com which version of the DKIM protocol we're using. So far, there's just one version of this protocol. But in the future, the protocol could be upgraded.

- a=rsa-sha256; This tells bob.com what kind of signature is being used. In this case, it's an RSA signature with an SHA-256 hash. We won't dig into the relative merits of this particular choice of algorithm. For now, we can be content knowing that alice.com has a way to specify the signature to be used for each outgoing email.

- c=relaxed/relaxed; This lets alice.com tell the other mail server that some minor changes to some of the headers could take place and that's ok. In this case, minor changes are things like capitalization changes and differences in whitespace.

- d=alice.com; This tells bob.com what domain is signing this email. Bob will use this when looking up the DNS record to verify the signature.

- s=aliceselector; The selector is a DKIM concept that lets bob.com look up the right DNS record. The selector and domain from this example would be used together to look up the TXT record for the following machine via DNS: aliceselector._domainkey.alice.com. More explicitly, the receiving mail server combines the selector + "._domainkey." + the domain to construct the machine name to query in DNS. We'd query that DNS record like this:

```
$ dig aliceselector._domainkey.alice.com txt

; <<>> DiG 9.8.3-P1 <<>> aliceselector._domainkey.alice.com txt
;; global options: +cmd
;; Got answer:
;; ->>HEADER<<- opcode: QUERY, status: NOERROR, id: 22673
;; flags: qr rd ra; QUERY: 1, ANSWER: 1, AUTHORITY: 0, ADDITIONAL: 0

;; QUESTION SECTION:
;aliceselector._domainkey.alice.com.    IN      TXT

;; ANSWER SECTION:
aliceselector._domainkey.alice.com IN TXT
"v=DKIM1\; k=rsa\; p=MIIBIjANBgkqhkiG9w0BAQEFAAOCAQ8AMIIBCgKCAQEAr2eLwRoQWz0Q
+HmrCTqTCpal1JR9TGDfO99TJ3P+X79mSBBaETUKNuJHqcQYurOkS1PY0B/
M8i3p7ebxavovEXGdHtl1oRNqLJ0An/3jxD9cmldq4/
PEkAtlmhkkAt0gpvq8uCmsIbOQe6hvUEKHzef0c73MG82jey1/yHdkYEnK0Q/
lJ45JPw/txIqxwsKAo"
"UpqlzVcz5YBJb2loD2xS6M7xxygmnuWb5ehXcW+
kXz8UiO5m9iMGF737KmCSS5GCWl/U7PYFpjxNnjJJEjlJCKDgz0pcD43VO+
UaSTydmaE7te590RYtS6Rw4rPr2uZAFIq7vn/X26d4/7XJ3SrpwIDAQAB"

;; Query time: 106 msec
;; SERVER: 192.168.0.1#53(192.168.0.1)
;; WHEN: Sun Jul  1 17:22:03 2018
;; MSG SIZE  rcvd: 472
```

bob.com would execute this domain query to get alice.com's public key and use it to verify the signature. Remember the p=MIIBIjANBg... part of that DNS entry. That's the public key, and bob.com is going to use it shortly.

- h=From:Date:Subject:Message-ID:Content-Type:MIME-Version; This is where alice.com specifies which email headers will be signed. Emails have lots of headers, and not all of them are signed.

- bh=f73482ef... This is the hash of the body of the email as calculated by the hashing algorithm specified by the a key/value pair. In our example, this is SHA-256. This header is used in the b= key, which we'll see next.

- b=3I9Ix/9Q... This is the signature of the headers specified by h along with the hash of the body of the email. Legitimate email from alice.com will be signed with alice.com's private key. Then, when bob.com verifies the incoming email, bob.com will take that signature and verify it using the the public key p=MIIBIjANBg.... that we just looked up with the DNS query. If the signature is valid, bob.com will trust the email. If it's not, bob.com won't trust it.

Knowing all this, we can see how bob.com can use a header like this to verify an incoming email that claims to have been sent by alice.com. In our example, Bob.com will follow these steps:

1. Look at a to see that SHA-256 is the hashing algorithm to use.

2. Construct the SHA-256 hash of the message body

3. Combine the message body hash and the headers specified by h.

4. Verify that bh is the signature of the value calculated in step 3.

Taken together, bob.com can use these steps to gain a fair amount of confidence that the incoming email is legitimate. If the incoming email were a forgery composed of bits and pieces of previous legitimate emails, the signature check would fail. If any of the fields specified by h had changed, the corresponding signature would have been different.

On the one hand, this is nice because it can provide guarantees about the origin of incoming email. On the other hand, this is fairly complex, and there are lots of opportunities for mistakes that would allow forged emails to slip through. This is another excellent reason to not manage an email server yourself. Let Google handle it for you. You don't want to have to rotate signing keys, or deal with any of this if you can avoid it. With G Suite you only have to check a couple boxes and add a public key to your DNS records and you're all set.

There are more options to DKIM configuration, but we've covered the parts you're most likely to want to use. For more details, see the DKIM website,[7] RFC 5585,[8] RFC 6376,[9] RFC 5863,[10] or RFC 5617.[11]

---

7. http://www.dkim.org/
8. http://www.rfc-editor.org/rfc/rfc5585.txt
9. http://www.rfc-editor.org/rfc/rfc6376.txt
10. http://www.rfc-editor.org/rfc/rfc5863.txt
11. http://www.rfc-editor.org/rfc/rfc5617.txt

DMARC

DMARC, or Domain-Based Message Authentication, Reporting, and Confor-
mance is another DNS-based email tool. It's built on top of SPF and DKIM
and has two main uses. First, it can be used to help troubleshoot complex
SPF and/or DKIM rules. Second, it can be used to collect forged emails for
later analysis. Let's take a look at the DMARC records in use for punkgrok.org.
We do this by looking at the TXT DNS records for _dmarc.punkgrok.org, as
follows:

```
$ dig _dmarc.punkgrok.org txt

; <<>> DiG 9.8.3-P1 <<>> _dmarc.punkgrok.org txt
;; global options: +cmd
;; Got answer:
;; ->>HEADER<<- opcode: QUERY, status: NOERROR, id: 16424
;; flags: qr rd ra; QUERY: 1, ANSWER: 1, AUTHORITY: 0, ADDITIONAL: 0

;; QUESTION SECTION:
;_dmarc.punkgrok.org.            IN      TXT

;; ANSWER SECTION:
_dmarc.punkgrok.org.    14400   IN      TXT
  "v=DMARC1\; p=quarantine\; rua=mailto:postmaster@punkgrok.org\;"

;; Query time: 123 msec
;; SERVER: 192.168.0.1#53(192.168.0.1)
;; WHEN: Sun Jul  1 12:43:59 2018
;; MSG SIZE  rcvd: 114
```

Let's take a look at what DNS tells us here. The part we're most interested in
is here:

> v=DMARC1\; p=quarantine\; rua=mailto:postmaster@punkgrok.org\;

Just like SPF and DKIM, we see a configuration that's specified by tags. And
again we see that the first tag is the version number.

The second tag in this example is the policy tag.

> p=quarantine

This tells the receiving mail server what to do with an incoming email that
fails validation. There are three valid values for this: none, quarantine, and
reject. Section 6.1 of the DMARC spec defines these three policies as follows:
(https://tools.ietf.org/html/rfc7489#section-6.1)

> None: The Domain Owner requests no specific action be taken regarding delivery
> of messages.

> Quarantine: The Domain Owner wishes to have email that fails the DMARC
> mechanism check be treated by Mail Receivers as suspicious. Depending on the

capabilities of the Mail Receiver, this can mean "place into spam folder," "scrutinize with additional intensity," and/or "flag as suspicious."

Reject: The Domain Owner wishes for Mail Receivers to reject email that fails the DMARC mechanism check. Rejection SHOULD occur during the SMTP transaction. See Section 10.3 for some discussion of SMTP rejection methods and their implications.

Next, we see rua, which stands for "reporting URI(s) for aggregate data." This lets the domain admin specify one or more email addresses to which aggregate reports of validation failures should be set. This functionality can be used to debug SPF and DKIM issues. This can also be used to analyze information about who is sending forged emails.

It's hard to find mistakes in configurations for DKIM or SPF because the DNS records that drive them are interpreted by servers owned by other organizations. If we mess something up, our outbound emails will just get dropped and we won't know why. With DMARC reporting, we can at least see what emails were getting dropped by other organizations and work backward from that to fix it. If there are problems with SPF and/or DKIM, it's common to encounter them when working with a third party that sends emails on your behalf, such as a marketing partner. If you want them to be able to send emails for you, you need to include them in your SPF and DKIM configurations. For one example of the kind of coordination problem that can pop up, consider what happens if your marketing partner changes their public IPs but you don't update your SPF records. When your marketing emails reach the recipients' mail servers, they'll check the SPF records, see that they no longer match, and your marketing emails will start getting dropped but you won't know why. With DMARC, you can find out what happened.

Another use of the DMARC report is to find IPs that are sending forged emails for your domain. You can't do much about it directly, but you can send the reports to spam clearing houses that maintain reputation scores for IP ranges and domains.

There are more options to DMARC configuration, but we've covered the parts you're most likely to want to use. For more details, see the DMARC website[12] or RFC 7489.[13]

---

12. https://dmarc.org/
13. https://tools.ietf.org/html/rfc7489

Authentication-Based Defense

So now we've trained current employees and added anti-phishing training as part of onboarding for new employees. We've used DNS-based defenses so that incoming phishing emails can't be forged to look like they came from our domain. What else can we do to defend ourselves? We've done everything we can do to decrease the likelihood of lost credentials. Now let's see what we can do to reduce the impact of lost credentials.

2FA

In a traditional login, a user supplies a username and password to authenticate themselves to the system. In this scenario, the password is the single factor the system uses to decide whether to authenticate the user or not. That works fine until the password becomes known to an attacker. This disclosure lets the attacker log in as a legitimate user. If the system had a second factor to be used in addition to the password, then disclosure of the password would not compromise the account. This is the idea behind two-factor authentication (2FA).

TOTP

The most common type of 2FA is a time-based one-time password (TOTP). In a TOTP system, the server and the client share a second secret in addition to the password. During login, after the user submits the password, the user uses the 2FA application, which uses the current time and the shared secret to generate the time-based one-time password. The user submits this second password, and the server, which knows the current time and remembers the shared secret, can perform the same derivation and make sure that the second factor is correct.

TOTP Limitations

Adding 2FA to our logins can provide some defense against phishing. An attacker might steal a username and password, but without the second factor, they can't log in. This stops the effectiveness of simple password theft and can make attempts to use the newly stolen password stand out. But, depending on the type of deception used in the phishing email, it might not be enough to stop a more sophisticated attacker.

Consider a phishing campaign where the phisher wants to exfiltrate data out of a web-based system that's protected by 2FA. All the phisher needs to do in addition to the normal credential stealing is to convince the user that they need to supply the second factor as well. This can be done with a Man-in-the-Middle style attack. The phishing email will contain a link to a login look-alike web page under the phisher's control, just as in a normal phishing email. This page will then steal the username and login, store it, submit those credentials to the legitimate login site, and present the user with a lookalike 2FA button. Since the legitimate login site received valid credentials, it will challenge the legitimate user with the 2FA challenge button. But in this scenario, the user already thinks they need to log in. They're expecting the 2FA challenge, so they supply the second factor, thinking that it's authenticating the login process they're seeing on their screen. But instead, it's authenticating the login process initiated by the phisher's website.

The presence of 2FA makes this attack harder to pull off. There are more moving parts, there is a second opportunity for the user to decide not to authenticate, and the legitimate website will know the IP address that the phishing site is connecting from, which could raise alarms. But these challenges for the phisher are only speed bumps. None of them actually prevent the attack.

Prefer Non–SMS-Based 2FA

There are a variety of 2FA options. Apps that run on your smart phone seem to be the most popular. Some of the smart phone-based 2FA apps communicate over SMS, which isn't ideal.[14] Phone companies can be social-engineered into making account changes.[15] And attacks on the cell phone network itself are possible.[16]

You're still much better off with SMS-based 2FA than with no second factor. But if you have the choice, pick a non-SMS system. Requiring 2FA for logins helps decrease the value of stolen credentials. It also helps in the face of credential-stuffing attacks.

U2F

U2F is a more advanced form of 2FA. It is an open standard designed to address a couple of the shortcomings of typical 2FA.[17] First, U2F is not phishable. Whereas a TOTP client trusts the server implicitly and hands over the TOTP automatically, a U2F client performs a handshake not unlike the TLS handshake. This lets the server and the client authenticate each other. If the server is an imposter (as is the case in phishing attacks), it will fail this authentication step and won't gain anything that will help it log in to the

---

14. https://www.wired.com/2016/06/hey-stop-using-texts-two-factor-authentication/
15. https://www.youtube.com/watch?v=lc7scxvKQOo
16. https://arstechnica.com/information-technology/2017/05/thieves-drain-2fa-protected-bank-accounts-by-abusing-ss7-routing-protocol/
17. https://fidoalliance.org/

> \/ / **Joe asks:**
> :,   **What Is Credential Stuffing?**
>
> Credential stuffing is an attack that targets password reuse. After a breach that results in a large number of leaked usernames and passwords, attackers can try those username/password combinations against other online services. This attack is effective because password reuse is so rampant that it's almost guaranteed that some of the username/password pairs in a large credential dump will be reused for other websites. It's also effective because it doesn't look like a brute force attack to defenders: it looks like a single failed login attempt for a targeted account. Legitimate users mistype their passwords all the time; you can't sound the alarm every time someone mistypes their password.
>
> For more information about credential stuffing, see the OWASP writeup.[a]
>
> ---
>
> a.   https://www.owasp.org/index.php/Credential_Stuffing_Prevention_Cheat_Sheet

website it's impersonating. Second, U2F clients are small, purpose-built devices. The most popular variety is the YubiKey line of U2F devices from Yubico.[18] They're generally about the size of a small USB thumb drive. They only have the ability to perform the U2F handshake. They don't have a full-featured operating system with the ability to run apps like a smart phone, so they're much harder for an attacker to compromise. Typical TOTP 2FA applications run on either a phone or a regular computer. If either the phone or the computer were to be compromised through targeted malicious software, the 2FA app could become compromised too.

If you have the option, choose U2F. There are a couple reasons it may not be the right option for you today, however. Though adoption is increasing, it's not supported on every platform just yet. Another downside is that it requires purchasing a small hardware device for every person in your organization. And then it requires that every person in your organization have this device with them whenever they want to use protected services.

In-Application Defense

Once you have 2FA in place, you'll definitely want to require it for login. In fact, 2FA at login time is what most people think of when they think of 2FA. But 2FA can also be required by applications before allowing particularly sensitive operations. Examples of sensitive operations include changing passwords, changing the email address used for the current account, and

---

18. https://yubico.com

transferring money. Requiring 2FA for sensitive operations means that even if an attacker got past the login 2FA (for example, by physical access to an unattended, logged-in computer, or by Man-in-the-Middling a TOTP login), the phisher would need to bypass 2FA a second time, which is difficult.

Another defense for highly sensitive operations is a four-eyes check. In a four-eyes check, two different people must give approval before a system will perform highly sensitive operations. These approvals are audited. This significantly raises the bar for an attacker.

The four-eyes check and the additional 2FA challenge are both strong defenses. Additionally, they are both noisy defenses. Attacks that are stopped by either of them leave behind clear, high-quality signals for later analysis. Unfortunately, they must be used sparingly because they carry such a heavy usability cost. They can only be added to the most sensitive operations.

If you use a cloud hosting service like AWS,[19] you'll want to protect your AWS admin accounts with 2FA. These account credentials are just about the most important data you have. If the credentials for these are leaked, or if the admins reuse credentials from another site that gets compromised, then attackers will be able to take over your entire cloud infrastructure.

Got Phished. Now What?

So what should we do if one of our colleagues gets phished? The first thing to reemphasize is to not tease or punish them. It's an easy mistake to make. The rest of the company will be watching, and the more scared they get, the less helpful they'll be in future incidents.

If you think an attack has taken place, contact your legal department right away. They'll coordinate communication with law enforcement.

You'll want to bring in an incident response company to help with the aftermath. Recovering from an attack like this is outside the scope of this book.

That said, there are some things that you can expect that an incident response company would want to be able to do as part of an incident response. To start with, they'll want to figure out what the phisher was after and how the attack was carried out. Generally, this will mean finding out what malicious website(s) the phisher used. Once you find this out, you'll want to block all access to that site at your firewall. Phishing is a numbers game, and it's likely that other members of your organization were targeted as well. You'll also want

---

19. https://aws.amazon.com

to find out whether any other members of your organization also clicked on the link. Hopefully you'll be able to find that out by looking at your firewall logs. Though if you have people who work remotely, you most likely won't be able to block their access to the malicious site and won't be able to know whether or not they went to that site.

Once you know who's visited the malicious site, you'll know whose accounts could have been compromised. Have them rotate their passwords. Next, you'll want to see what their account has done since they visited the malicious site. It can also help to find out if any accounts have recently logged in from IP addresses they haven't logged in from before. You'll also want to see who has logged in from the same IP as those used by the accounts of the people who visited the malicious site. This can provide another clue as to whose accounts have been compromised. If you have a single-sign-on provider, you'll have a much easier time finding this out.

The last couple paragraphs assumed a lot of infrastructure was already in place. If you don't have these tools in place, set aside some time to think about how you'd carry out an investigation without them. If the answer is that you wouldn't be able to do much of an investigation if you didn't have them, then you'll probably want to budget some time and money to get those tools in place before an attack happens, rather than afterward.

For more on responding to phishing incidents, read Ryan McGeehan's essay "Phishing Incident 101"[20] at his website, Starting Up Security.[21] You'll find many other useful essays there as well.

Wrapping Up

That's it. We've covered five basic areas to start your security efforts: patching, software vulnerabilities, cryptography, Windows, and phishing. Getting these in order will close the door on some of the most common attacks. This will also help you get the most out of the security experts you work with.

There is a lot more to security than what you've learned in this book. You'll likely want to incorporate practices like monitoring and static analysis as you bring in security staff and grow your security program. The linked books and websites in this book will help you dig deeper into these topics.

Remember that knowing the basics is just the start for effectively securing your systems. Good luck.

---

20. https://medium.com/starting-up-security/phishing-incident-101-863cbd4c1676
21. https://scrty.io/

Bibliography

[DMS06]   Mark Dowd, John McDonald, and Justin Schuh. *The Art of Software Security Assessment*. Addison-Wesley, Boston, MA, 2006.

[Kim18]   Peter Kim. *The Hacker Playbook 3: Practical Guide To Penetration Testing*. Independent, Everywhere, and nowhere, 2018.

[SP11]   Dafydd Stuttard and Marcus Pinto. *The Web Application Hacker's Handbook*. John Wiley & Sons, New York, NY, 2011.

Thank you!

How did you enjoy this book? Please let us know. Take a moment and email us at support@pragprog.com with your feedback. Tell us your story and you could win free ebooks. Please use the subject line "Book Feedback."

Ready for your next great Pragmatic Bookshelf book? Come on over to https://pragprog.com and use the coupon code BUYANOTHER2019 to save 30% on your next ebook.

Void where prohibited, restricted, or otherwise unwelcome. Do not use ebooks near water. If rash persists, see a doctor. Doesn't apply to *The Pragmatic Programmer* ebook because it's older than the Pragmatic Bookshelf itself. Side effects may include increased knowledge and skill, increased marketability, and deep satisfaction. Increase dosage regularly.

And thank you for your continued support,

Andy Hunt, Publisher

Fix Your Hidden Problems

From technical debt to deployment in the very real, very messy world, we've got the tools you need to fix the hidden problems before they become disasters.

Your Code as a Crime Scene

Jack the Ripper and legacy codebases have more in common than you'd think. Inspired by forensic psychology methods, this book teaches you strategies to predict the future of your codebase, assess refactoring direction, and understand how your team influences the design. With its unique blend of forensic psychology and code analysis, this book arms you with the strategies you need, no matter what programming language you use.

Adam Tornhill
(218 pages) ISBN: 9781680500387. $36
https://pragprog.com/book/atcrime

Release It! Second Edition

A single dramatic software failure can cost a company millions of dollars—but can be avoided with simple changes to design and architecture. This new edition of the best-selling industry standard shows you how to create systems that run longer, with fewer failures, and recover better when bad things happen. New coverage includes DevOps, microservices, and cloud-native architecture. Stability antipatterns have grown to include systemic problems in large-scale systems. This is a must-have pragmatic guide to engineering for production systems.

Michael Nygard
(376 pages) ISBN: 9781680502398. $47.95
https://pragprog.com/book/mnee2

Secure JavaScript and Web Testing

Secure your Node applications and see how to really test on the web.

Secure Your Node.js Web Application

Cyber-criminals have your web applications in their crosshairs. They search for and exploit common security mistakes in your web application to steal user data. Learn how you can secure your Node.js applications, database and web server to avoid these security holes. Discover the primary attack vectors against web applications, and implement security best practices and effective countermeasures. Coding securely will make you a stronger web developer and analyst, and you'll protect your users.

Karl Düüna
(230 pages) ISBN: 9781680500851. $36
https://pragprog.com/book/kdnodesec

The Way of the Web Tester

This book is for everyone who needs to test the web. As a tester, you'll automate your tests. As a developer, you'll build more robust solutions. And as a team, you'll gain a vocabulary and a means to coordinate how to write and organize automated tests for the web. Follow the testing pyramid and level up your skills in user interface testing, integration testing, and unit testing. Your new skills will free you up to do other, more important things while letting the computer do the one thing it's really good at: quickly running thousands of repetitive tasks.

Jonathan Rasmusson
(256 pages) ISBN: 9781680501834. $29
https://pragprog.com/book/jrtest

JavaScript and more JavaScript

JavaScript is back and better than ever. Rediscover the latest features and best practices for this ubiquitous language.

Rediscovering JavaScript

JavaScript is no longer to be feared or loathed—the world's most popular and ubiquitous language has evolved into a respectable language. Whether you're writing frontend applications or server-side code, the phenomenal features from ES6 and beyond—like the rest operator, generators, destructuring, object literals, arrow functions, modern classes, promises, async, and metaprogramming capabilities—will get you excited and eager to program with JavaScript. You've found the right book to get started quickly and dive deep into the essence of modern JavaScript. Learn practical tips to apply the elegant parts of the language and the gotchas to avoid.

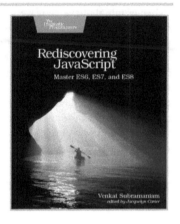

Venkat Subramaniam
(286 pages) ISBN: 9781680505467. $45.95
https://pragprog.com/book/ves6

Simplifying JavaScript

The best modern JavaScript is simple, readable, and predictable. Learn to write modern JavaScript not by memorizing a list of new syntax, but with practical examples of how syntax changes can make code more expressive. Starting from variable declarations that communicate intention clearly, see how modern principles can improve all parts of code. Incorporate ideas with curried functions, array methods, classes, and more to create code that does more with less while yielding fewer bugs.

Joe Morgan
(282 pages) ISBN: 9781680502886. $47.95
https://pragprog.com/book/es6tips

Python, too!

For data science and basic science, for you and anyone else on your team.

Data Science Essentials in Python

Go from messy, unstructured artifacts stored in SQL
and NoSQL databases to a neat, well-organized dataset
with this quick reference for the busy data scientist.
Understand text mining, machine learning, and network analysis; process numeric data with the NumPy
and Pandas modules; describe and analyze data using
statistical and network-theoretical methods; and see
actual examples of data analysis at work. This one-
stop solution covers the essential data science you
need in Python.

Dmitry Zinoviev
(224 pages) ISBN: 9781680501841. $29
https://pragprog.com/book/dzpyds

Practical Programming, Third Edition

Classroom-tested by tens of thousands of students,
this new edition of the best-selling intro to programming book is for anyone who wants to understand
computer science. Learn about design, algorithms,
testing, and debugging. Discover the fundamentals of
programming with Python 3.6—a language that's used
in millions of devices. Write programs to solve real-
world problems, and come away with everything you
need to produce quality code. This edition has been
updated to use the new language features in Python
3.6.

Paul Gries, Jennifer Campbell, Jason Montojo
(410 pages) ISBN: 9781680502688. $49.95
https://pragprog.com/book/gwpy3

The Pragmatic Bookshelf

The Pragmatic Bookshelf features books written by developers for developers. The titles continue the well-known Pragmatic Programmer style and continue to garner awards and rave reviews. As development gets more and more difficult, the Pragmatic Programmers will be there with more titles and products to help you stay on top of your game.

Visit Us Online

This Book's Home Page
https://pragprog.com/book/rzsecur
Source code from this book, errata, and other resources. Come give us feedback, too!

Keep Up to Date
https://pragprog.com
Join our announcement mailing list (low volume) or follow us on twitter @pragprog for new titles, sales, coupons, hot tips, and more.

New and Noteworthy
https://pragprog.com/news
Check out the latest pragmatic developments, new titles and other offerings.

Save on the eBook

Save on the eBook versions of this title. Owning the paper version of this book entitles you to purchase the electronic versions at a terrific discount.

PDFs are great for carrying around on your laptop—they are hyperlinked, have color, and are fully searchable. Most titles are also available for the iPhone and iPod touch, Amazon Kindle, and other popular e-book readers.

Buy now at *https://pragprog.com/coupon*

Contact Us

Online Orders:	*https://pragprog.com/catalog*
Customer Service:	*support@pragprog.com*
International Rights:	*translations@pragprog.com*
Academic Use:	*academic@pragprog.com*
Write for Us:	*http://write-for-us.pragprog.com*
Or Call:	+1 800-699-7764